Bending Towards Justice

*'The arc of the moral universe is long,
but it bends towards justice.'*

~ *Martin Luther King Jr*

I have known Nils for a couple of decades, and have never met a more 'readable writer'. We have many things in common: both employed at various times by World Vision; both worshipped for a while at St Martin's in Collingwood; both enjoyed walking along bush tracks together to 'rearrange the universe' from time to time; and we each have a concern for the poor and less-privileged (and writing about it).

Reading this manuscript distracted me for more time than I'd set aside for the task. And the outcome? I'll be putting this readable book on my Christmas wish-list this year!

Rowland Croucher
John Mark Ministries
(Author of the 'Questions & Responses' series,
published by Coventry Press)

These reflections are gentle and challenging, pointing us always toward the transforming love of God. For me, this short series is a timely appeal to justice, grace and the discovery of real humanity.

Rev'd Dr Bob Mitchell
Chief Executive Officer
Anglican Overseas Aid

Passionate and profound, this series of essays takes the reader on a journey of what it means to be a follower of Jesus in today's consumeristic and indifferent world. Placing justice firmly at the heart of the Gospel message, Nils' focus on the personal transformation that all who follow Christ must undergo is nothing short of a call to action, challenging us all on how we are each participating in the life-transforming, redemptive work of bringing Christ's Kingdom to Earth. It's a timely message for a world that remains in desperate need of the hope the Gospel brings.

David Adams
Editor, Sight Magazine

This beautiful collection of pithy articles addresses a wide range of profoundly significant topics with considerable insight and a refreshing lightness. Much of the subject material is grim reading, but at heart the book is one of hope. Why? Because, as the author says: 'God is on the move. Rumours of hope are breaking out all over the world'. The articles and stories in this book testify to the truth behind those rumours. Read one chapter a night before going to sleep and you will be strengthened by that hope.

Steve Bradbury
Director, Micah 6:8 Centre
Eastern College, Australia

BENDING TOWARDS JUSTICE

How Jesus is more relevant than ever in the 21st century

NILS VON KALM

COVENTRY
PRESS

Published in Australia by
Coventry Press
33 Scoresby Road
Bayswater Vic. 3153
Australia

ISBN 9780648497745

Copyright © Nils von Kalm 2019

All rights reserved. Other than for the purposes and subject to the conditions prescribed under the *Copyright Act*, no part of this publication may be reproduced, stored in a retrieval system, or transmitted in any form or by any means, electronic, mechanical, photocopying, recording or otherwise, without the prior permission of the publisher.

Unless otherwise noted, Scripture quotations are from the *New Revised Standard Version Bible*, copyright 1989, Division of Christian Education of the National Council of the Churches of Christ in the United States of America. Used by permission. All rights reserved.

Cataloguing-in-Publication entry is available from the National Library of Australia http://catalogue.nla.gov.au/.

Cover design by Ian James - www.jgd.com.au
Text design by Megan Low, Film Shot Graphics (FSG)

Printed in Australia

Contents

Acknowledgments 9
Introduction 11
A Christmas Reflection 15
A Dream Awakened... 18
A Lenten Reflection... 23
A Story of Transformation 26
A Time for Being Still 28
A Vision of Home... 31
Advent and the Strange Man from the Inner City.......... 34
An Easter Blessing.. 38
Count It All Joy?!!! 41
Does It Really Matter What We Believe? 45
Ending Poverty: This Is Personal....................................... 48
Footy With Phuong – Meeting My Sponsored Child...... 51
Freedom from Indifference... 54
God is a Materialist 57
Good News for the Rich – That's Us................................ 62
How to Become More Popular in Three Easy Steps 65
Imagine.. 68
Jesus and Women 71
Jesus Makes an Appearance in the Morning Rush 74
Jesus of Australia.. 77
Living the dream 81
Love and the Facebook Hug Vest 83
Love in all its Fullness... 87
Reverend Billy and the Church of Stop Shopping.......... 90
Sharing Fruit to End Poverty... 93

Sport as a Reflection of the Dream of God 95
Stand for Something or Fall for Anything 99
Successful Social Movements 101
The Best is Yet to Come 104
The Disarming Beauty of Grace 107
The Eternal Question 110
The God of Suffering Love 113
The Grace-Filled Life of Brennan Manning 115
The Great 'R' Word - Renewal 119
The Inherent Value of Work 121
Was Jesus a Tree-Hugger? 123
What does Prayer have to do with Poverty? 126
Your History Doesn't Have to be Your Destiny 132
Recommended reading 136
About the Author 139

Acknowledgments

It is difficult to think of who to acknowledge when there are so many who have had such an influence on my life.

The thoughts and reflections in this book arise out of a lifetime of inspiration for which I am literally eternally grateful.

I need to first thank World Vision Australia, with whom I worked for 14 years. They gave me the opportunity to do what I love: write about the links between Christian faith and all of life. This book would not have been written if it wasn't for World Vision.

John Smith (founder of God's Squad), Martin Luther King, and Bono of U2 are the three people who have probably had the greatest impact on me. Their passion for Jesus, their courage and genuine expression of faith are what I have always wanted to emulate.

Gandhi, Bobby Kennedy, Oscar Romero, Mother Teresa, John Mellencamp, Midnight Oil, Larry Crabb, N.T. Wright, and Richard Rohr are others who have contributed to who I am today. If only they knew how grateful I am for that.

Closer to home are people like Morris Stuart, Jon Fraser, Simon Fee, Shirley Osborn, Lorraine & Claud Johnstone, Rowland Croucher, Peter Saunders, and Tim Costello. Each of them in their own way has helped me want to be a better man.

Bob Mitchell and Brian Holmes provided detailed editing and fine tuning of the ideas. I also thank them for their warm friendship during some difficult years in my life.

Bending Towards Justice

Then there are the unsung ones, the ones who are too many to name here but who have had more of an influence on me than they know. These are the friends of mine who are not mentioned above, the people who give their lives for the cause of goodness, who just love what they do and do it with love. They are humble, sacrificial and just really good people. You are my heroes.

Finally - and I don't mean this in any obligatory way at all - is Jesus himself. When I committed my life to him as a reserved teenager, I didn't understand what I had done. But I wouldn't be here without him. I believe he is who the Gospels say he is. After 35 years, I am still fascinated by him. He shapes my life, gives me meaning, and is transforming me into the person I have always wanted to be: my true self. I will never be thankful enough for him.

To all these people, I thank you from the bottom of my heart.

To all those people who have influenced me over the years, whether public figures or people I know personally. My life is richer because of you.

Introduction

'Then I saw a new heaven and a new earth; for the first heaven and the first earth had passed away, and the sea was no more. And I saw the holy city, the new Jerusalem, coming down out of heaven from God, prepared as a bride adorned for her husband. And I heard a loud voice from the throne saying,

'See, the home of God is among mortals. He will dwell with them; they will be his peoples, and God himself will be with them; he will wipe every tear from their eyes. Death will be no more; mourning and crying and pain will be no more, for the first things have passed away.' And the one who was seated on the throne said, "See, I am making all things new".'

~ Revelation 21:1-5

Christians believe that the universe has a purpose. The Good News is that, through Jesus Christ, God is renewing this world and has given us the privilege of participating in that. What we participate in now has eternal significance and will one day be fully completed.

With God's people as co-creators of this new creation, all of existence will one day be transformed into one of love, justice and peace. The universe is bending towards justice, and it is all because of Jesus.

Jesus called this new creation the kingdom of God. It was so important to him that he spoke about it more than anything else. The kingdom is mentioned over a hundred times in the gospels.

Bending Towards Justice

All of Jesus' stories, whether parables or real-life events, pointed to this thing called the kingdom of God. Frustratingly for some, Jesus never defined the kingdom; he never said, 'this is what the kingdom is...' Instead, he pointed to it by describing what it was like, and what it looked like. And of course in his life, the people saw the kingdom coming alive. Just as he said in Luke 17, the kingdom was indeed among them.

The power of Jesus' message lay in many things, not least his very person; however, it was the genius with which he used the power of story that pulled people in.

Jesus spoke in a language that people could relate to. In an agricultural society he talked about mustard seeds and yeast. In a world in which cultural divisions ran to extremes, Jesus took them further and used them to show the supremacy of love. In his most famous parable of all, the Good Samaritan, he makes the Samaritan the hero. His parables were shocking, offensive, and yet delightful to those who had ears to hear.

While Jesus spoke in a language that the people of his time understood, for us in the 21st century it can be a lot harder. We simply can't relate to mustard seeds and Samaritans in our urban, 24/7 lives. The best way for us to understand what Jesus meant by the kingdom of God is to translate it into a language we can understand today. And just like Jesus showed, the best way to do that is not to define it specifically, but to point the way, to say, 'it is like...'

The privilege of being Christian doesn't lie in the fact that we have a ticket to a spiritual place called heaven when we die. Contrary to much of what goes down for Christian teaching, Jesus never actually spoke about a place like that. He was much more interested in heaven coming here. That is what he meant when he talked about the kingdom.

For Jesus, heaven is nothing other than the rule and reign of God. As the leading New Testament theologian, N. T. Wright, says, we can describe the rule and reign of God by asking, 'what would it be like if God were running the show?'

So, what would it look like? Well, because Jesus tells us no less than eighty-seven times in the gospels to follow him, it's best to look where Jesus went so we can follow him there. More than anything else in the gospels, Jesus was known as a friend of sinners and outcasts. The poor and oppressed were those who heard him gladly. It follows then that going where Jesus went, being sent to where he was sent, means doing the same as him.

The privilege we have in following Jesus is going out into all the world and bringing in this new reign of God.

The articles in the following pages are my thoughts gleaned over years of working for a Christian aid and development organisation. For some years now, I have been incredibly fortunate to be doing what is pretty much my dream job. Most people can't say that, so I regularly remind myself to be grateful for what I have. I'm grateful that my job involves writing about how Christian faith is relevant to the struggles that most of the world goes through on a daily basis.

And the struggles are plenty. While there has been much progress in terms of the alleviation of global poverty, the world is currently in a state of fear and uncertainty the likes of which have never been seen in human history.

In Western nations alone, loneliness is an epidemic, depression has increased tenfold since the Second World War, and climate scientists tell us that the globe is warming at a faster rate than even they had anticipated. This is all happening during a period in which we have never been richer economically (despite significant global downturns in the last decade). Something is wrong.

Into this global environment, we hear the words of Jesus down through the ages. Commands to love God and neighbour (which will at times include our enemies), warnings about greed and that life does not consist in the abundance of possessions, warnings about losing our identities while we obsess over enormous riches. Jesus and his message are more relevant now than they have ever been.

Many of the articles in this book focus on the conditions of people in the majority poor world. But they also focus on life in the affluent West, where I was born and live. Through an accident of birth, my life is privileged. I am a white, middle-class male, living in one of the richest countries in the world. I have never known what it is to live in poverty; I have never known what it is to not know where my next meal is coming from. I live in a comfortable house, have a good job, and enough money to do almost anything I want in life.

Most of the world doesn't live like I do. So these articles are as much a reminder to me as they hopefully will be to you, that our lives do not consist in the abundance of our possessions, but in surrender to the One who gives us everything we have in life.

In reading this book, it is my hope that you will be edified, encouraged and challenged to follow Jesus more closely, to love him more dearly, and to more resolutely take up the fight against evil in this world. If we do that, then love, justice, peace and joy – all attributes of God – will invade and take over the world, as Jesus said, like yeast spreading through dough.

I am convinced that there is a God who loves each and every one of us, regardless of race, religion or gender. I also believe we are made in the image of this God to go into all the world and bring the reign of God to bear. May this book inspire you to do just that.

A Christmas Reflection

The movie *Joyeux Noel (Merry Christmas)* tells the amazing true story of the Christmas truce that took place on Christmas Eve, 1914, between British, German and French soldiers in the trenches on the Western Front in World War 1.

During this part of 'the war to end all wars', soldiers from opposing sides who were stationed there to kill each other, instead fraternised, got to know one another, shared photos of loved ones, and even had a game of soccer.

This, of course, made their superiors furious, not just because the troops were disobeying orders, but because it is much harder to harm someone with whom you have formed some sort of relationship. The enemy is to be faceless and nameless.

Working in international aid and development, you soon realise that the enemy that is poverty is not faceless. As Global Leader on Faith and Development for World Vision, Jayakumar Christian, has said for many years: people are the issue, not just poverty.

Poverty is about people bleeding; it is not about numbers. Poverty is not an 'issue'. These are people's lives we are talking about. Christian goes on to say that poverty is also not just a lack of material things; it is about a lack of dignity, a lack of a sense that you are important. Ash Barker, founder of Urban Neighbours of Hope, talks about this when he reminds us of the imperative to make poverty personal. It is about getting to know them. Alleviating poverty is about relationship.

Back in the year 2000, the World Bank undertook a major study of poverty from the point of view of those actually experiencing it. In the study, called *Voices of the Poor*, 60,000 poor people were asked what poverty was for them. The overwhelming response was that it was about lack of power, lack of dignity, and that it drives one into despair.

At Christmas, we celebrate the coming of God to Earth in the form of a human, Jesus Christ. Also known as the Prince of Peace, Jesus came to set the world to rights. In *The Message* translation of the Lord's Prayer in the Gospels, Jesus' prayer is written as,

> 'Our Father in heaven,
> Reveal who you are.
> Set the world right;
> Do what's best – as above, so below.'

The more common translation that many of us would be familiar with includes the phrase, 'may your kingdom come on earth as it is in heaven'.

This kingdom of God is something that Jesus talked about more than anything else. It is a kingdom of transformation, and it is transformation of the physical, the emotional, and the spiritual. It is transformation at every level.

In the last book of the Bible, Revelation – a book that is often difficult to understand – it is described in terms of a promise that there will one day come a time when God will consummate this kingdom and that God will then 'wipe every tear from their eyes. There will be no more death or mourning or crying or pain, for the old order of things has passed away' (Revelation 21:4). Justice, peace and transformation will prevail. This is the promise that we have from the One who was born as a helpless baby in a manger 2,000 years ago.

Jesus made poverty personal. He saw everyone he came into contact with as a person of dignity. People who met him were never the same again. They were transformed in every way. This is God's vision for the world.

Everything about who we are as believers - our very identity - is wrapped up in who Jesus is and what he has done - God coming to earth to identify as one of us, to bring good news to the poor, to set the captives free and to restore the world to rights. This is the dream of God, and it is the hope of Christmas.

A Dream Awakened

In Matthew 6:9-13, Jesus teaches his disciples how to pray. What follows is the model for the most famous prayer of all – the Lord's Prayer.

In this prayer, Jesus tells us to pray for God's kingdom to come on earth as it is in heaven. Throughout the rest of the gospels, Jesus then goes on to mention the kingdom of God no less than a hundred and ten times.

What is this kingdom of God that Jesus constantly spoke about? Depending on the churches you go to, or what you may have heard throughout your life, there are different understandings of the kingdom of God which generally fall into the following categories:

- Heaven when we die
- The church
- The reign of God starting now but fully consummated when Jesus returns

Based on the character of God revealed throughout the Bible, the kingdom is the reign of God that started with the coming of Jesus and which will be fully realised when he returns.

The characteristics of the kingdom reflect the character of the King (God). The Bible tells us that God is a God of love, justice, peace, humility and compassion. God is good. Therefore, the kingdom of God fully realised will be a place where these characteristics (along with many other good ones as described in Isaiah 58) reign supreme.

A kingdom of transformation

If we want a closer look at what this kingdom looks like, we can look at the life of Jesus in the gospels. In Luke 17:21, Jesus says to the Pharisees (the religious establishment of the day), 'the kingdom of God is among you'.

Jesus was making the outrageous claim that in him, this kingdom of God has broken into history. The gospels tell us that Jesus healed people. He showed compassion to those rejected by most of society, he stood up for what was right and just, and he cared for people regardless of their ethnicity, race or religion. The kingdom involves words and actions of love, transformation and justice being made real in the here and now.

When Jesus prays for the kingdom to come on earth as it is in heaven, he wants us to have the privilege of being a part of it, of bringing transformation to every part of existence. This includes our spirituality, our politics, our economics, our finances, our sexuality, our morality, and our environment.

The bottom line is love – love for God and love of neighbour. As our neighbours throughout the world most often happen to be the poor, and as Jesus is revealed in the gospels as a friend of the poor and outcast, following him means we have the privilege of going and doing likewise.

When we say that Jesus is a friend of the poor and outcast, it does not mean that he loves them at arm's length. Jesus made poverty personal. His approach to people is always relational; it is always about identity. It was not about statistics for him, which is what we often make it today.

The transformation of Zacchaeus

Consider the story of Zacchaeus, told in Luke 19:1-10. Zacchaeus, though rich beyond measure, was also seen as 'less than', being a hated tax collector. But after Zacchaeus forgoes his cheating ways by paying back four times the amount that he has ripped off from people, Jesus makes the bold claim that 'salvation has come to this house'. Zacchaeus is transformed in every way, and his transformation involves his performing an astonishing act of justice.

When our hearts are transformed by Jesus, we want to live out that transformation in the world. And conversely, as we live out that transformation in the world, our hearts are further transformed.

What is God's will?

Martin Luther King once said that the end of life is not to be happy but to do the will of God. The will of God is to follow Jesus.

In John 20:21, Jesus says 'As the Father has sent me, so I send you'. Jesus was sent to bring good news to the poor and to liberate the captives (Luke 4:18). This does not mean just the physically poor and it does not mean just the spiritually poor. In Jesus' day, such dualistic thinking did not exist. In fact, in Hebrew, which Jesus would have known, there is no word for 'spiritual'. Life was one seamless garment, not something that was compartmentalised into different areas.

To follow Jesus is to be a disciple. In the gospels, Jesus says eighty-seven times to 'follow me'. This and the kingdom of God are what he spoke about more than anything else. And our job is to continue what Jesus did in living lives of transformation. This transformation is perhaps best summed up by New Testament theologian N. T. Wright:

'God is on the move and we are invited to be a part of it. Life is going somewhere. God is transforming the world, healing the world. God's new creation has begun and we get to be part of it.'

We are God's representatives here on earth. In what we call the Great Commission (Matthew 28:18-20), we are called to go and make disciples, to go and make people who follow Jesus into the laneways and the by-ways of life, to the poor and discarded ones, to those who believe they have no worth and have lived their lives accordingly. We are to bring them abundant life in every way, being Christ to them, embodying our Saviour in all we are and do.

Outbreaks of hope

We have the privilege of providing outbreaks of hope, outbreaks of the kingdom, through our lives. The kingdom of God has come in the life, death and resurrection of Jesus, and it continues to come through his Spirit working in those who follow him today.

Every act of kindness, every act of justice, every act of grace we perform, matters. It will exist in the kingdom to come, that wonderful day when all will be made new, when all will finally be consummated, when there will be no more tears and no more pain, when the old order of things will have passed away (Revelation 21:4).

This will be the day when heaven and earth join together fully, when the curtain is finally pulled back to reveal the wonder of God's glorious new creation. On that day, the creation itself will have been liberated from its bondage to decay and brought into the glorious freedom of the children of God (Romans 8:21). Everything will have been transformed, and it will all be because of Jesus. And the great news for us is that we get to be a part of all this.

As we live out this kingdom life, we realise that we live in the creative tension of the 'now and not yet'. The kingdom is here and yet the kingdom is waiting to be fully revealed at the end of all things. This is our great hope. As Eden Parris sings in his song, *Deeper Magic*,

> *Have you heard on the wind distant murmurs of spring?*
> *They say Aslan is on the move*
> *And the people in caves are beginning to pray*
> *They say that he will be here soon*
> *To banish the night and to make all things right*
> *To colour the earth with his song*
> *But the most precious thing is it's already spring*
> *It was buried right here all along*

God is on the move. Rumours of hope are breaking out all over the world. The kingdom is here and the kingdom is coming. What a privilege to be a part of something so big that it swallows up our own dreams and awakens something deep within us where we find what we have always been looking for.

A Lenten Reflection

If you are walking around in a supermarket not long after Christmas, you could be forgiven for thinking that you had skipped a couple of months of your life, such is the proliferation of chocolate Easter eggs already for sale. We are a society addicted to consumption. We want it all, and we want it now.

The temptation to succumb to the consumerist way of life is with us daily. So it is always time to remind ourselves that Jesus faced the same temptations we do. In Luke 4, we read that Jesus was shown all the kingdoms of the world, in all their glitz and glamour, and was told it could all be his if he would just sell his soul. Those forty days in the wilderness for Jesus were a time of extreme testing and trial.

Jesus resisted all the temptations thrown at him during that time, because he knew a better way. Not an easier way, but a better way. What the gospels show us is that the way of Jesus is the way of the cross. In his day, that meant nothing less than a death sentence. When Jesus told his disciples about this in Mark 8, it was the major turning point in his ministry. It was the beginning of the end. Sometimes referred as the Caesarea Philippi Declaration, this was the first time Jesus made clear to his disciples that he was going to go to Jerusalem to meet his death.

What we also see in this enormously significant passage is that the disciples just didn't get it. How could they? They had a completely different mindset. Their idea of a messiah was one who would overthrow the tyranny of the Roman Empire. After all, that was something that the Jews had been pinning their hopes on for hundreds of years. They had been under the yoke of oppression for that long and they had had enough. So when Jesus came along and spoke to his disciples about self-denial and taking up your cross and that he was going to die, should we be surprised that they couldn't deal with it?

We need regular reminding that following Jesus is a struggle. When we commit our lives to him and to bringing in the kingdom of God in all we are and all we do, it can be easy for cynicism to easily take hold as we see corruption and injustice always seeming to win the day. How do we go on when it always seems to be two steps forward and three steps back?

Jesus, though, walks before us and prepares us for what lies ahead. He helps us to identify with suffering, with going without, in order to realise more our dependence on the God of hope.

In a world where we constantly face the temptation to want it all and want it now, Jesus offers a different way. The way of Jesus is the way of the cross. It is an unavoidable fact of life. There is no resurrection without death.

Sacrifice can not only bring us closer to God, but it can also help us identify more with those whose entire lives consist of going without. And by doing this, you may just find that you experience a joy that you would not otherwise experience; a joy that can give you strength to continue the good fight.

As author Walt Wangerin says, 'Joy knows suffering and still does not despair. Joy sees the suffering of others and does not turn away, but moves forward in courage, to comfort and to heal'.

The prophet Nehemiah also says, 'the joy of the Lord will be your strength'. Jesus knew this. He knew it on the night he was betrayed and we can be sure he knew it during his forty days in the wilderness.

Nils von Kalm

The journey of struggle to set the world right is a long one. But it is one that brings life and joy, and that is why it is worthwhile. May that be your experience of following Christ.

A Story of Transformation

As a Christian, I gain my motivation and inspiration primarily from the life of Jesus. I long to be transformed into the image of Christ, to be more Christlike in my character.

Transformation for me includes transformation of everything in me and in my world. It ranges from the ravages of injustice to the flowing streams of justice, from the wretchedness of poverty to the beauty of dignity, and from the ugliness of a self-centred life to the fragrant attraction of a life lived for others. As Jesus said, the kingdom of God is like yeast working its way through the dough. It is an outbreak of love, as *Midnight Oil* sang years ago, and it cannot be stopped.

Perhaps the most complete example of transformation in the gospels is the story of the woman with the flow of blood in Mark 5:24-34. This event, like any in documents such as the gospels, needs to be taken in context.

Picture the scene: there are people everywhere. By this stage of his public life, Jesus had rock-star status. The crowds were all clamouring around him, pushing and jostling him.

Now consider the woman. First, being a woman in that society meant you were a second-class citizen, and your testimony wasn't valid in a court of law simply because of your gender. Secondly, she had had haemorrhages for twelve years, meaning that she was most likely unable to have children, which also meant she was probably divorced. In those days, you were considered cursed by God if you couldn't have children, and a husband could easily divorce his wife for that reason.

This woman didn't have a lot going for her. In short, she was a social outcast. No wonder she was so timid that she could only put a finger on Jesus' robe. She had such a low sense of self-worth that the terror of being noticed was too much for her.

What we see then is a couple of incredible events. First, the woman is healed physically. After all the years of dealing out money to unscrupulous doctors who left her worse off than before, finally something had changed in her body and she knew it.

Then we have Jesus asking the seemingly bizarre question of who touched him, when there were people crowding him in on every side. Why does Jesus ask who touched him? Because mere physical healing was not what Jesus was on about.

As the woman comes forward in fear and trembling, we see her social and spiritual healing. Jesus affirms her in front of everyone; and he does it by calling her 'daughter'. This woman, who has been defined by others and by herself as 'less than', is now told by Jesus that she is included. She is one of the family. Imagine what this does for her. She is now no longer a pariah; she has been restored as a normal member of society.

This story highlights the type of transformation I want to see in the world. It is transformation at every level of existence: our society, our hearts, our politics, our economics, our morality, and our environment. It is a transformation of love, and it is inspired, motivated, and energised by the life, death and resurrection of Jesus himself. We are truly fortunate people, working to help bring in the kingdom of God on earth. As Richard Rohr says, transformed people transform people. May it continue to be so in my life.

A Time for Being Still

In our 24/7 culture, where we feel a debilitating anxiety if we don't have our smartphones with us, more and more people are realising the need to take time to be still and reflect on our lives and what we are here for.

Mindfulness has become the latest way for people to be still. Contemplation is crucial for our mental health, as it frees us from anxiety and helps us be present in the moment.

There is something in us that craves time for stillness in our busy lives. No matter what we are going through, we always benefit from taking time to stop and reflect. In fact, semi-regular contemplation is actually guaranteed to make you happier and improve your relationships.

Contemplation and meditation have often been viewed with suspicion in some Christian circles. Many Christians believe that, if we empty our minds, we leave them open for demonic activity to take place. Personally, I think such fears are well overstated. There are clear emotional, physical, mental and even spiritual benefits to mindfulness. What we do need to be careful of, though, is that we don't practise mindfulness as a substitute for being close to God. Life is ultimately found in attachment to God, surrender to the only One who can free us from our fears and selfishness. If we use mindfulness as a process of detachment instead of attachment, that is indeed detrimental to our wellbeing.

Overall though, the practice of mindfulness, contemplation and meditation actually has its roots in the Hebrew scriptures. In Psalm 46, we read the edifying words, 'Be still and know that

I am God'. What the Psalmist is talking about here is not just the psychological benefits – though there are many – of taking time to be still within our busyness. He is actually talking about taking time to reflect on the character of God.

The world we desire as Christians is a kingdom that reflects the character of the King. The Bible gives various descriptions for God, none more evident than that God is loving, compassionate, merciful, just and relational. The world we are working towards is one with these characteristics. Psalm 46 refers to these traits, describing God as our refuge and strength, and a solid rock amidst the storms of life. When we take the time to ponder this, it gives us strength to go back out and do more than is humanly possible.

Jesus himself needed time for this kind of reflection. If he did it, then who are we to say it is dangerous? And it wasn't just prayer that Jesus practised. Not prayer as in talking to God anyway. He spent whole nights in communion with his Father. This would have also included listening and contemplating and being still, as the Psalmist says. We see instances of this in Matthew 14:23 and 26:36, as well as Mark 1:35, Luke 5:16 and John 6:15.

What we see in these passages is that Jesus thrived on his connection with God. It was his sustenance. For example, during his wilderness experience, Jesus gained strength from remembering that people do not live on bread alone, but on every word that comes from the mouth of God.

Contemplation can take different forms, and it is often the forms that originated in the Roman Catholic and Orthodox traditions that many people find most useful. The *Stations of the Cross* is one example that is used, mainly in the lead-up to Easter, to reflect on Jesus' Passion – his suffering during his final hours on earth. Then there is *Taize*, which is a service of prayer and meditation that both Roman Catholic and Protestant traditions use. It includes music and simple chants, often from the Psalms, as well as icons from the Eastern Orthodox tradition.

When we take on this type of contemplation in an attitude of submission to God, we find that we grow more into the likeness of Christ. One of the paradoxes of Christian faith is that we become more human, more the people we were born to be, when we surrender our lives to God's will. This is what Jesus did in the Garden of Gethsemane on that terrible night before his crucifixion. Jesus was human just like us; he was tempted – and wanted – to take the easier way, just like we often do. But his response was one of surrender – 'not my will but yours be done'.

We do our best work when we have this attitude of surrender and soak it in prayer and contemplation. Some of the best advice on this comes from Franciscan priest Richard Rohr: 'When either waiting or moving forward is done out of a spirit of union and surrender, we can trust that God will make good out of it – even if we are mistaken! It is not about being correct; it is about being connected'.

Connection is what the human soul ultimately longs for. As Rohr goes on to say, it is our connection, or relationship, with God that leads to the radical works of justice with which we are engaged.

It is through contemplative stillness on the love and grace of God that we are empowered to continue the good fight without becoming bitter and burned out. It is only when we surrender our wills to God that we become transformed people who transform the world.

A Vision of Home

In the movie *Avatar*, the main character, Jake, comes to sympathise with the native Na'vi people who are facing the demolition of their home by humans in search of a precious metal. As Jake gets to know the Na'vi, he eventually empathises with them so much that he becomes one of them.

Latin American theologian, Ruth Padilla DeBorst, has spoken of what she calls the hopeful distance of God. She says that God is not off in some far-off place called heaven looking down on the mess of a sick world. Instead, God is right next to us. Like Jake in *Avatar*, God has empathised with us so much that he actually became one of us. In *The Message* version of the Bible, we are told in John's Gospel that 'the Word became flesh and blood and moved into the neighbourhood'. Earlier, we are told that 'the Word' is God. In the person of Jesus, God has moved into the neighbourhood. God is our neighbour, someone who wants to get to know us and befriend us. God wants to make his home with us.

Many people have described coming to faith in Christ as a coming home. It has often been described as finding what you have been looking for all your life (sometimes even when you didn't realise you were looking). Everyone is on a search for life, for something better, something outside of ourselves. As *Midnight Oil* sang back in the '90s: 'Where is home? Where is my home? I'm searching far and wide'.

The Bible talks about home as being the Promised Land that God led the Israelites into. Ultimately, this Promised Land is the completely renewed creation that God is creating for us as we speak. On 3 April, 1968, the night before he died, Martin Luther

King spoke passionately about his people getting to the Promised Land. For him that meant freedom for African Americans who had been oppressed for centuries under the ugly yoke of racism. But he was also alluding to that day when all of God's children would live together in harmony in the new world that was King's dream.

In 1963, Dr King's dream became famous. The *I Have a Dream* speech so eloquently describes the new world that King and his people longed for. As King thundered out to the hundreds of thousands of people watching, this dream was not just the American dream, it was not just a dream for African Americans; it was a dream for everyone, which everyone is invited to be a part of.

The Promised Land that King longed for was the home that God has made for all people. The crucial point to remember though is that when we talk about a new society – a new order if you like – this thing called the kingdom of God; it is not just about a harmonious society. It is more like a loving, close, intimate family. It is a place where you know you belong, a place where, when you think of it, you think of the word 'home'.

When Ruth Padilla DeBorst spoke about the intimacy of God, she was talking about connection. She was really talking about relationship. It is about ultimate things. She was talking about a God who is always right beside us. Years ago, Joan Osbourne sang 'What if God was one of us?' Well, God already is. We are never alone. The sense of never being alone is ultimately what we all crave.

But where is home for the asylum seekers kept by the Australian Government at the Manus Island Detention Centre in Papua New Guinea for example? Are we more concerned about border protection than human protection? Are we more fearful of the stranger than welcoming of the stranger? Love is not fearful; perfect love drives out all fear. Love is freedom.

In the name of Jesus, we try to welcome the stranger, give bread to the beggar, and provide hope for all. For those who have suffered the affliction of addiction to drugs which have now given them HIV, or who have indulged in sexual practices that now have them suffering the scourge of this terrible disease; to these people we offer not judgment but hope and healing, love and compassion. That is what Jesus does. Jesus does not condemn the sinner; if he did, he would have to condemn all of us the same. Instead Jesus welcomes us, bids us home.

For the prodigal son, who wasted his life, and as he was out in the dirty laneways of a far country, eventually realised what his life had come to; to people like this Jesus not only welcomes, he actually runs out to meet us as we trudge the long weary road back home.

We feel unworthy of any welcome at all, and would not be surprised one bit if Jesus told us he had had enough and the door was firmly slammed in our face. The surprise we get though is completely the opposite. We get the surprise of the most extravagant welcome possible as the food is piled on and the party begins, all for us.

What kind of God is this who welcomes the one who has gone astray, the one who has let everybody down? What kind of God is this who leaves his ninety-nine sheep to go out and search for the one who was lost? It is the God of Jesus, the God we try to follow and in whose shoes we try to walk.

Our goal is to try to be like this Jesus, to bring the lost one home, to bind up the broken hearted, to release those who are captive to all the things that bind their life. Whether it be addiction, poverty, abuse, exploitation, or any kind of injustice, this Jesus is the one who comes to release and save.

Advent and the Strange Man from the Inner City

Did you hear in the news the other day about this guy who has appeared in the streets of the inner city? He's really weird. Apparently he wears tattered jeans, a torn flannelette shirt and loves eating nothing but tofu at one of those hippy cafes in the area. Not the sort of bloke that any self-respecting middle-class office worker would want to mix with.

And – get this – he also walks up and down the streets yelling obscenities about the current Government and major retailers and how they have led our state into nothing less than an addict's cauldron of consumerism and materialism that has completely blinded people to the true meaning of Christmas. He then goes on about how he has a vision for something better than all that. Typical bleating of a nobody from the poor inner-city.

The thing is, though, that what this bloke (who calls himself simply 'John') says makes sense in an odd sort of way. You wouldn't think anyone from the inner city who looks like that would be worth listening to, but apparently the Premier went down there with some of his Cabinet team the other day, and was even joined by the CEOs of David Jones, Calvin Klein and Pumpkin Patch. They'd heard about this John and couldn't resist having a look at what all the fuss was about. But when John saw them, man he let fly! He looked them in the eye and told them, 'Just because you live in comfortable houses and get paid really well and work hard for your money, don't think you have any sense of entitlement to the good life!'

What a nerve this John has! Who does he think he is, talking to powerful and respected people like that?! Sooner they take him off the streets the better.

Despite his whining, though, John has gained huge popularity in the last few weeks with his loud warnings of the danger to come if we keep going down the way of this consumerism stuff. The YouTube clip of him has gone viral. Many people try to avoid him, though, and more and more retailers are trying to have him banned from going into the central city area during December. Fair enough too; you can't have a public nuisance like that disturbing people's Christmas shopping. Retail sales would plummet and the economy would collapse. And then where would Christmas be? Thank God for our Premier and those CEOs doing their job of keeping us all comfortable.

The above story is, of course, fiction. It is a modern-day parable of a John the Baptist-type figure. John the Baptist was that fiery strange prophet referred to in some of the Gospels. He lived out in the desert, thought that clothes made from camel hair was good dress sense, and that a diet of locusts and wild honey was satisfying. Today he would be the sort of person we would probably stereotype as being from the inner city and yelling at passers-by.

An appropriate description for the Christian Gospel is that it comforts the afflicted and afflicts the comfortable. It is both comforting and disturbing at the same time. This comes out in spades in the story of John the Baptist.

The thing that confronts us about John the Baptist is that God chose this weird, loud, hairy prophet above all the great rulers of the time to announce the greatest event in the history of the world. A little passage tucked away in Luke's Gospel shows us the stark distinctions between who God sees as important and what the prevailing culture does. While all the great rulers were strutting their stuff, God speaks through an unknown recluse in the desert. Don't you love that?

Bending Towards Justice

The story of John the Baptist reminds us that we have sanitised the Christmas story so much that today's version would be near unrecognisable to most people from the 1st century. As another John – John Smith, founder of God's Squad – has said, John the Baptist was born into an atmosphere of disillusionment, heartbreak, weariness and wonder, and it is through such circumstances that God speaks to us, not through our happy times.

John the Baptist spoke about God's mercy to the powerful elite of his day. He gave them practical advice when they asked him for it: if you have two shirts, give one away; if you have enough food, do the same (isn't that challenging to us as we fill our stomachs to the brim at Christmas!). He said all this to the people who were the respected ones of his day. As John Smith goes on to say, the message of John the Baptist speaks against anyone who wants to stand in solidarity with power and privilege.

Coming into the time of preparation for Christmas – the time many Christians call Advent – it is humbling to remember the stories of people like John the Baptist. For instance, another little obscure verse in Luke's Gospel confronts those of us who have thought that simply believing the right things is what it's all about. After the story of what John the Baptist was doing, Luke 3:18 says, 'with many other words John exhorted the people and proclaimed the good news to them'. What John the Baptist was saying when he advised people how to change their behaviour was the Good News, none other than the Gospel. The Gospel is not about intellectual belief. It is love in action.

John the Baptist shows us what being a Christian is all about. It is not about believing the right things. It is not just about being born again. A faith that stops there is not real faith. Real Christian faith transforms your character from within and impacts the world around you.

God is found in unexpected places. Looking at the Christmas story at Advent, the thing we will learn is that God is not found in the things of power and status; God is instead found with the poor and lowly, the ones who are shunned by polite society. We will also learn that life is not found in the comforts of our material existence, but is found in suffering and hardship. And if you run into a strange wild man in the inner city in the next few weeks, stop and have a listen to him. You might just be brought closer to Jesus.

An Easter Blessing

We live in a world of immense suffering, and whether we call ourselves Christian or not, we are often faced with the universal question of why such suffering occurs in a world that was made by a good and loving God.

At Easter, we remember that when Jesus was dying on the cross, he also asked why, and then said 'into your hands I place my spirit'. It was an act of trust that God is good despite what we see around us.

In our society, we are bombarded with the message every day that life is found in having more. Gordon Gekko's 'greed is good' mantra from the heady days of the late 1980s is the philosophy we are encouraged to live by today. Yet study after study shows that 'money can't buy me love', as The Beatles sang more than fifty years ago.

The American psychologist, Martin Seligman, has conducted research showing that the rate of depression in Western nations has increased tenfold since the Second World War. This means we now have *ten times* the number of people who are depressed than we had seventy years ago.

On top of that, Brene Brown points out that we are the most in-debt, obese, addicted and medicated people in history. All this is during a period in which we have never been wealthier. Something is not adding up; it looks suspiciously like we have been sold a lemon.

And if that is not enough, our affluent way of life is leading to a greater gap between rich and poor, as well as to the dreaded spectre of a changing climate. The former National Director of World Vision India, Jayakumar Christian, says that while everybody talks about the booming Indian middle-class, with economic growth rates of 7-8%, no one talks about the growing gap between rich and poor in that vast land, and the fact that there are hundreds of millions of poor people in India.

And if you read about what is happening in places like Africa, you will learn about the effects that climate change is already having on their farming practices. No wonder the author and pastor Brian McLaren calls our way of life the 'suicide machine'.

It's all depressingly bleak, and enough to drive you to despair. But despite all this, we don't have to be stuck in that mindset. The comfort we can find at Easter is that Jesus identifies with our pain and with our questions. And it's more than that. If that is all he did, we wouldn't have any hope. Thankfully, we are told that in Jesus, God came to earth not only to die for our wrongs, but to reconcile all things to himself.

But again, if that is all there is, there still wouldn't be any hope. The New Testament is open about this. The apostle Paul says that if Christ was not raised from death we are to be pitied more than anyone. Christian faith lives or dies on the physical resurrection of Jesus as a historical event.

If Jesus was not raised, then Christian faith is pointless, as death would not have been defeated and life is meaningless. But our joy and hope come from faith in Jesus, that as well as dying on Good Friday, he was raised on Sunday. As Nick Cave sings, death is not the end. And, as only he can, American preacher Tony Campolo adds, 'it's Friday but Sunday's a-comin!'

Hope is alive. There is no line on the horizon; heaven and earth are slowly overlapping. There is no reason to despair and there is nothing to fear. The Christian message says that it is because of the resurrection of Jesus on that first Easter morning that we have hope that death will not triumph in the end. Life, justice, peace, hope and love will triumph. Nothing is surer. And it is all because God came and dwelt among us and defeated the scourge of death.

Through the life, death and resurrection of Jesus, we are shown how to live, we are offered forgiveness for our many wrongs, and all things are reconciled to God. *All* things. Our hearts, so we can be at peace with God; our society, so we can live at peace with each other; and the rest of the whole created order, so we can live at peace with it.

To the question of why God doesn't seem to be doing anything about the suffering and pain in the world, we can assuredly say that God already has. Through the life of one man, we see a glimpse of the wonderful kingdom come; through the death of that one man on a dark Friday afternoon, we are offered forgiveness for our wrongs; and through the resurrection of that one unique man on the most wonderful Sunday morning in history, all things are made new.

What we remember at Easter is what drives us; it is what drives our continual struggle for a better world, for peace on earth, for shalom. One day, there will be no more tears; one day, there will be no more pain, no more 'stupid poverty' as Bono calls it, no more war and no more injustice. One day everything will fit; it will all make sense. And it will all be because of Jesus. And we get to live this resurrection life here and now, working with God to renew the world, living out the compassion of Jesus, and standing in the tradition of the prophets to work for a world in which one day everything will be made complete. That is the hope of Easter.

Count It All Joy? !!!

The Letter of James in the New Testament seems at first glance to have been written by a sadist. Who in their right mind would open a letter by saying, 'Consider it pure joy, my brothers and sisters, whenever you face trials of many kinds' (James 1:2)?! The writer is either completely lacking in tact or just doesn't understand what people who are suffering need to hear.

But what if there was another way of understanding what James is saying? What if we looked at this letter in context and realised that James, like his brother Jesus, was in fact very familiar with suffering and was actually giving courage to the readers of his letter?

Our culture has lost the idea of what joy is. We either talk about it in sarcastic terms, like when we say 'Oh joy!' when something goes wrong, or we might hear *Joy to the World* sung at Carols by Candlelight on Christmas Eve, or we equate joy with happiness, as seen on some TV commercials for particular products. Only rarely will we hear joy being talked about in its proper context, like when we hear or see something about the 'joy of giving'.

A culture that worships pleasure, success and the pursuit of happiness as much as we do is not going to be interested much in joy as the Bible describes it. This is because joy comes out of an inner attitude that exists despite our circumstances. When we try to minimise any type of pain in our lives and live with the goal of feeling good, we cannot know joy.

Don't misunderstand this. This is not about being masochistic and going out looking for suffering. To the contrary, it is actually about living in reality. Sometimes life just sucks and there is nothing we can do to change it. Maturity is, then, about dealing with life on life's terms, not demanding that it give us what we want.

The affluent world lives with a spiritual and relational poverty. This type of poverty is primarily born out of our demand that life gives us what we want; it comes out of the goal of pursuing happiness and pleasure as the ultimate in life. The tragic irony is that it has produced the most alarming social disruption and decay we could imagine.

We read articles in the newspapers about how Australians are turning inward, becoming fearful and complaining that life is so bad. Yet we are pretty much the only Western country that got through the Global Financial Crisis of 2008 without a recession, our unemployment is still around 5%, and we have one of the lowest levels of debt of any affluent economy in the world.

Could it be that our grumpiness, despite such a high standard of living, is a result of our pursuit of happiness? A culture that is fixed on an unsustainable goal is one that is never satisfied. Like the 1st Century Roman proverb that says 'Money is like seawater: the more a man drinks, the thirstier he becomes,' our thirst for more and better is insatiable, keeping us forever dissatisfied. On top of that is the old truism that the more you have, the more you fear losing it.

We pursue happiness by trying to control our lives to get the maximum benefit for ourselves and our loved ones. Joy though is different. Joy is what we can have whether life goes our way or not. It is the unexpected by-product of being free from the burden of working so hard to control our lives. Happiness is fleeting, joy is lasting. To maintain happiness we always have to do something more or buy something else. Maintaining joy involves living in reality.

If we wanted the best example of joy in suffering, it would make sense that we would look for it not just in the ultimate Source of joy, but in a way that we humans can relate to. This is exactly what we have in the man Jesus. Do you know the only time in all four gospels that Jesus talks about his own joy? Here are some clues from the famous piece, *One Solitary Life*:

> *His friends ran away*
> *One of them denied him*
> *He was turned over to his enemies*
> *And went through the mockery of a trial*
> *He was nailed to a cross between two thieves*
> *While dying, his executioners gambled for his clothing*
> *The only property he had on earth*
> *When he was dead*
> *He was laid in a borrowed grave*
> *Through the pity of a friend*

All of this happened in a period of about twenty-four hours, and it is during these most excruciating twenty-four hours that anyone has ever had to experience that Jesus says to his disciples in John 15:11, 'I have told you these things so that my joy may be in you, and that your joy may be complete'.

Jesus shows us that joy is not happiness. At Easter each year we see this displayed in his life in the ultimate way: there is no resurrection without death.

The whole New Testament was written in a context of suffering. If you are suffering at the moment, you are in good company. God suffers too. Christian faith is not about nice teaching that tries to console us when life hurts; it is about a God who actually comes down into our distress and sits with us, cries with us, relates to us. It is deeply personal.

The deepest human need is for love and understanding. The Christian story is about God giving us exactly this. Jesus gets his hands dirty and forsakes all for the sake of others. This is love in action, it is love linked with joy, because it is love born out of gratitude that we are not alone in our suffering.

Does It Really Matter What We Believe?

Why do so many Christians care about alleviating poverty and working for justice in the world? Put simply, what is our theology, and does it really matter?

Theology in itself is the study of God and of God's relationship to everything else in existence. For some people, theology conjures up images of people in ivory towers poring over books and doctrine and other things that don't seem anywhere near related to the realities of life on the ground. But it is crucial that we have our theology right. It matters what we believe.

Much of the theology we hear in our churches is basically individualistic, Western, and focuses ultimately on saving souls and getting people into heaven. Within this worldview, the alleviation of poverty and working for justice are seen as good things to do, but they are not as important as saving souls, because people's eternal destiny is what really matters in the end. The other stuff is just temporary.

Such theology is not biblical. It actually has more to do with Enlightenment thinking than being from the Bible. During the Enlightenment, faith became more of a private matter and therefore had nothing to say about social, economic and political issues. If we look at the themes of the Bible, though, we see that it is ultimately a story. It starts with creation, follows the history of God's people as they stumble through the centuries, centres on the coming of God (in Jesus) into the world to start the process of getting things back on track, and ends with the final renewal of creation. And we are given the awesome privilege of being the instruments through which God renews the world. In the process, we are also renewed. This is the essence of the Gospel.

The reason this is so important is because if we get our theology mixed up, it can have tragic consequences. Take the case of Rwanda. At the time of the 1994 genocide during which 800 thousand people were killed in a few months, Rwanda was 94% Christian. How could a country in which almost everyone is Christian allow 800 thousand of its own people to be butchered like this? The reasons are complex, but part of it is because of a theology that was ultimately concerned about getting people into heaven and which therefore had very little to say about life in the here and now.

When we see the Bible as the story that it is, we see that it actually has nothing to do with who will end up with God forever in a disembodied place called 'heaven'. Such thinking is simply not biblical and misses the mark of who Jesus is, why he came and what his mission was.

Like all great stories, the end of the Bible is worth the wait. Revelation is probably the most misunderstood and misinterpreted book in the whole story. Ironically though, it is also the book that contains such good news about what creation's eternal destiny really is. In Revelation 21:1-4, we read that at the end of all things, heaven and earth will be joined forever, and God will dwell amongst God's people here in a new earth.

Do you see what this is saying? It is not about ultimately 'going up to heaven'; heaven is coming here! And when it is finally joined with earth, there will be justice for all; there will be no more poverty, no more tears and no more pain. And the best thing: no more death.

Ultimately, it is the resurrection of Jesus that is the basis for this hope. This is a hope that is based on something that actually happened in history – that God came to earth in Jesus, he died and was physically raised from death, never to die again. Because of this, our work is not in vain.

I believe in transformation, transformation of the here and now, in anticipation of, and contributing to, the ultimate transformation when the curtain is fully drawn, the full glory of heaven is revealed on earth and our deepest desires are fully realised. It matters that what we believe is biblical, as this fuels our passion to work with God to renew this broken world.

Ending Poverty: This Is Personal

One of the main distinctives of Christian faith is that it sees God as a Trinity. We talk about God the Father, God the Son, and God the Holy Spirit: one God in three persons. It is something the human mind can't fully get its head around, but it is central to our belief in a God who is relational.

Psychologist Larry Crabb refers to God as the Eternal Community. It is in this way that we see God as both ultimate and intimate. The Bible tells us that God is love, and love at its essence is about giving. So for love to be expressed, it must be given away. And the only way this can happen is within relationship.

This is why Jayakumar Christian, the former National Director of World Vision India, says that poverty is about relationships. In his book, *God of the Empty-Handed*, he says that 'poverty is not about numbers. It is about inequality, and specifically about inequality in power relationships'.

Poverty, according to those who are living it, is primarily about lack of power and lack of dignity. The poor are the powerless and we, the rich in the West, are the powerful. It is about a relationship, a relationship that is unequal. Jayakumar goes on to say that poverty is about 'real people who experience hurt, pain, disappointment, love and compassion'. It is personal and is therefore intimately linked to relationship.

There is a wonderful painting called *Rublev's Icon* that portrays the relationship within the Godhead beautifully. If you look at it closely, you can see that all three persons are equal. They are all special and none is expendable. They are also different yet the same; their unity and diversity are respected. Additionally, they all share the one chalice. Because of all this there is stability and security. And at the front there is room for more. It is an open and welcoming community.

This is what the kingdom of God is all about. It reflects the very character of the Triune God. And because we are made in the image of this God, the very essence of being human is to be relational. This is why any attempt to alleviate poverty has to be relational. To try to alleviate poverty in a non-relational manner is to deny the humanity of the very people you are trying to help.

This is also why – and we must be careful not to misunderstand this – we must see any work to make a better world not as a 'cause'. Seeing it as simply a cause can take away the relational nature of it, strip it of its very core. Being true to who we are means having a mindset that thinks about everything in terms of relationality. The author Frank Viola says,

'It's possible to confuse "the cause" of Christ with the person of Christ. When the early church said 'Jesus is Lord', they did not mean 'Jesus is my core value'. Jesus isn't a cause; he is a real and living person... Focusing on his cause or mission doesn't equate [to] focusing on or following him.'

It is when we are captivated by Jesus himself that working to end poverty has its full impact. It is then that we find ourselves awakened to the dream of God which is deep within the heart of every one of us. It is then that we realise that the kingdom of God is personal and social all at the same time. As Viola goes on to say, the Jesus who came to inaugurate this kingdom 'cannot be separated from his teachings'.

Of Jesus it can truly be said that the medium is the message. He embodies his teachings. To be Christian is to be about the embodiment of transformation. When we embody Christ in everything we do, something deep within us is touched. Through our lives, the dream of our relational God is being awakened. We see it in little sparks in many different corners of the world, in the form of transformed relationships both within and between communities, and between people and their environment.

Eventually these sparks will turn into a raging bonfire that will consume everything that is wrong with the world, leaving only what is good, right and just: the renewal and restoration of all relationships in the universe, reflecting the ultimate Relationship, the Eternal Community of the One who made it all.

Footy With Phuong — Meeting My Sponsored Child

> Here's where we gotta be
> Love and community
> Laughter is eternity if joy is real
>
> (U2, Get on Your Boots)

There is something about children that brings a beautiful, disruptive joy to our busy lives. When we interact with children, we invariably gather around and smile and talk to them as if we were children ourselves.

No wonder Jesus said the kingdom of God belongs to such as these. The innocence, wonder and trust of a child teach us what is important in life, what really matters at the end of the day. It is a glimpse of eternity where love, community, laughter and joy will all be constant realities.

Love and community are ultimately what Christian faith is about. Research shows that the first five years of a person's life are the most important. It is those earliest years that set the child up for what type of person they will be, and for how they will see themselves and the world.

One of the great privileges I have had in my life occurred some years ago when I met my World Vision sponsored child, Phuong, in Vietnam. I had been sponsoring Phuong since 2004 and had been receiving updates about him over the years, so it was with much anticipation that I woke up on the morning of our visit to finally see him.

Bending Towards Justice

The community where Phuong lives is in central Vietnam. When we arrived, we were introduced to the World Vision staff. These people are amazing. Their dedication and commitment to their work remains through all sorts of hardships. Observing the quality of the relationships between the World Vision staff, the children and the teachers at Phuong's school was a highlight.

Then the big moment came – it was time to meet Phuong. I felt a combination of excitement and nervousness as I approached the school where he was waiting. As I got closer to the school gate, one of the World Vision staff pointed him out, waiting with a few of his little mates. I immediately went up to him and introduced myself, almost falling over myself to greet him.

After the greetings were done, I was marched straight to the Principal's office. That sounds ominous I know; the last time that happened to me I was in about Grade 4 and just about to get the strap for breaking some silly school rule! None of that this time though. The greetings I received from the Principal and other staff were incredibly welcoming. I found out that the funds I and many others are donating each month have helped to refurbish Phuong's school to the point that it's now able to welcome children from all over the district. The school has also won awards for its level of education.

It was being introduced to Phuong's mother though that made me realise how much this meeting of sponsor and sponsee meant to everyone there. She thanked me for my support, but without wanting to sound overly modest, the impact our contribution was making really didn't sink in. To Phuong's mother though, it was more than financial help; this was giving her son a life. It was that that made the impact on her.

After spending quality time with Phuong's mother and the staff of the school, I was invited to a quarterly birthday celebration the school puts on for all the children. Singing *Happy Birthday* and playing games with the children was a delight. I was told that many parents and children from the highland communities in the area don't know when their birthday is, so the quarterly birthday celebrations they put on for the children is very much appreciated by them.

I was then led outside to play with some of the children. This was my chance to hand over a gift I had brought over for the community. Many sponsors give a soccer ball to their sponsored child's community, to highlight the universal language of the world game. Being from Melbourne though, I thought I would do something different and bring over a little AFL footy for the children to play with. After almost breaking a window in teaching them how to kick (there's a reason my AFL career never really made it past the backyard at Mum's!), they all got into it as they learned to kick and chase this strange shaped ball as it bounced all over the place.

Meeting Phuong, his mother and his community made for an unforgettable day. It showed again the value of not just giving financially, but of creating and maintaining relationships with people from different walks of life.

There is something about humanity that makes us wired for relationship. We bear the imprint of our Maker, the God who is Parent, Son and Holy Spirit, whose very essence is relationship. Deepening my relationship with Phuong that day gave me a glimpse of the reign of this God, where laughter is eternity and joy is real.

Freedom from Indifference

Author Brian McLaren says that the great social movements in history have had spiritual foundations. Movements led by William Wilberforce, Gandhi, Martin Luther King, and Desmond Tutu, to name just a few, have had Christian faith at their core.

All these people had a vision for a better future, based on the life and teachings of Jesus (in case you are wondering, Gandhi wasn't Christian but he was influenced hugely by the Sermon on the Mount. He called it the greatest teaching ever given).

What happens, though, when in a grossly affluent society like ours, we are removed from the pain of the majority world? We cannot imagine a better future unless we feel the pain of the world now. One of the problems of our culture is that, on the whole, when it comes to issues of poverty and injustice around the world, we suffer from apathy. Out of sight, out of mind. As Walter Brueggemann writes in his classic *The Prophetic Imagination*, in our affluent culture we have become satiated to the point of indifference. One of the points he makes is that, 'it is difficult to keep a revolution of freedom and justice under way when there is satiation'.

It is my belief that this distraction from reality we encounter in our culture is a reflection of lost foundations. A society that moves away from its faith tradition, as our society has largely done, is a society that has lost hope. So, we watch so-called reality TV, and we enter the next lotto draw in the faint hope that more money will fill that nagging void within us.

It is often our artists who need to bring us back to reality with a prophetic word. Groups like U2 who sing 'I feel numb.

Too much is not enough', and Crowded House, who sang years ago, 'In the paper today, tales of war and of waste, but you turn right over to the TV page', and movies like *The Hunger Games* series illustrate how our entertainment culture keeps us from seeing life as it really is for the majority of the planet. As Soren Kierkegaard has said, we are 'tranquilised by the trivial', numb to the pain of a broken world.

The result of such living is that we have lost our ability to tell stories about our past, the great stories of what gave us our foundations. Brueggemann goes on to say, 'human transformative activity depends on a transformed imagination. Numbness does not hurt like torture, but in a quite parallel way, numbness robs us of our capability for humanity'.

We live in an addicted society that tranquilises pain wherever possible and so distracts us from envisioning a better world. To embrace the Gospel, though, is to embrace pain and suffering in the world. In a paradoxical way, it is through embracing pain that we encounter joy and life. It defies everything we are taught about how to live in our culture. And it is always a battle. There are principalities and powers out to destroy the work that we do. Whether you believe in a spiritual realm or not, I am convinced that evil exists in the world. There are powerful interests at play, and they must be challenged.

Despite these interests, the words of John in the New Testament speak truth to power in a way that nothing else can. We have Jesus saying in the day or so before his murder, 'In the world you will have trouble, but take heart, I have overcome the world'. In 1 John, we read that 'the One who is in you is greater than the one who is in the world'. And possibly the most powerful words from the writer of John's Gospel are about God invading the world with goodness. In John 1:5 we read the inspiring words, 'the light shines in the darkness, and the darkness has not overcome it'. If that doesn't move us as Christians, then perhaps that is a sign that we too have become tranquilised by the trivial.

Nothing makes you come alive more than committing yourself totally to something bigger than yourself. And it is a transformed imagination, the renewing of our minds, that does it. When people band together in a social movement with spiritual foundations, the world changes. The reason I soak myself in the Christian Scriptures is because in them I find purpose and reality. C. S Lewis once said, 'I believe in Christianity as I believe that the sun has risen: not only because I see it, but because by it I see everything else'.

In a world that often doesn't make sense, we are often tempted to give in to the seductions of the bright lights of our consumer culture. When this happens, let us be reminded that Jesus faced this as well. When many of his followers walked away because it was all too hard, he asked his closest friends if they wanted to leave as well. Peter replied in words that have countered the discouragement of millions throughout the ages: 'Who else would we turn to? You have the words of eternal life'. It is this that gives us the power to be free from indifference.

God is a Materialist

Saying that God is a materialist will immediately raise eyebrows for a lot of Christians. Such a statement ('God is a materialist') can be seen in two ways.

One is that it is an oxymoron, because materialism is seen as the idea that there is nothing in existence beyond the material, so to talk of God, a non-material being, doesn't make sense. It's like talking about a square circle.

The other way this statement can be seen is in the sense of a prosperity doctrine where God will bless you materially when you follow him.

It probably does not need any explaining to say that neither of these descriptions of this statement is what I am referring to when I say that God is a materialist.

So what am I saying?

Let me ask you a question. Do you believe you're going to spend eternity up in heaven with God? I recently asked that question in a talk I gave on this topic, and almost half the audience put their hands up.

Let's get this straight right from the start. Despite what we hear in many of our churches and despite what we sing in many of our church songs, our final destiny is not up in heaven with God. It's actually much better than that.

Most of us have either grown up with or are still told in our churches that the spiritual is more important, and has greater value than, the physical or material world.

Linked with this, many of us have had ingrained into us that our ultimate destiny is to go to heaven when we die to spend eternity with Jesus.

Such an idea has seen Christian faith become irrelevant for many, especially in a culture which is as comfortable for most people as Australia is. When you have it ingrained into you that it is ultimately about being saved and going to heaven, then your faith hasn't got anything meaningful to say to issues of poverty, justice, politics and economics.

With the Church preaching such a message for so many years, it is no surprise that we see Australian Census results over the last twenty-five years showing that fewer and fewer Australians are identifying as Christian. On top of that, more people are mocking the religion they've been exposed to. (Did you know that the number of people identifying as 'Jedi' in the 2016 census was 48,000?).

If you do a search on Google Images of 'heaven', the vast majority of images you will see are those of stairs reaching up into the sky, and people on clouds. When Christians have a belief that that is our final destiny, it becomes natural that we then focus our energies on saving souls – getting people into heaven, and by implication, avoiding the other place.

Such a belief not only short-changes the Gospel; if it is true, then we can be so bold as to say that God hasn't done his job. What we find, though, is that Jesus and the rest of the New Testament actually have very little to say about going to heaven when you die.

The fact is that God loves the material world. Matter matters to God. After all, God made it and said over and over that it was good. And if God says it is good, then who are we to deny its goodness by living our lives as if it's not that good?

Nils von Kalm

The overarching theme throughout the whole of the Bible is that God is in the business of making *all things* new. When Jesus says this, what part of 'all' aren't we getting? This earth, the whole created order, will one day be made new. Everything we see and touch and feel today will one day be renewed, including our bodies. It is in this sense that God is a materialist.

God loves the physical, and says it is no less valuable than the spiritual. In fact, God doesn't even separate the spiritual from the physical like we do. That idea is more of a Western construct than a biblical one.

We can be assured that the works we do now in our efforts of justice and poverty alleviation are not in vain. We are not fighting for a better world which will one day be destroyed while we escape off to heaven and leave it all here to rot, as too many Christians still believe.

We are also not fighting a losing battle, where the wicked and the corrupt always win. One day, the tables will be turned; the first will be last and the last will be first. There will be a day when there will be no more tears and no more pain, because those things will all be of the past. That is the great hope we have, and the great news is that we get to be a part of it right now.

We have the privilege of following Jesus into the places of poverty and injustice, into the places where the oppressed, the downtrodden, the troubled, and the addicted, are offered healing. It is a revolution of love that overthrows the current world order. The Canadian singer Bruce Cockburn calls it kicking at the darkness 'til it bleeds daylight.

If you can remember back to the first Gulf War in 1991, President Bush senior talked about creating a 'new world order'. Thankfully, it never came off, for it was to be an order based on military might where the rich and powerful dominate the weak and vulnerable. How different to the new world order that Jesus inaugurated. To the might and power of military imposition, we hear the quiet words of the Scriptures: 'not by might, not by power, but by my Spirit, says the Lord'.

The kingdom that Jesus spoke about and lived is a new world order that has already begun and will one day be completed when God finishes the job. It will be an order where all will experience justice, not just a privileged few. The privilege we have, though, is that we get to participate with God in renewing the world.

That is why everything you do in this life matters. Every act of kindness, every act of care you partake in every day, matters. It matters not just to the people who receive your kindness, but it matters to God and it has eternal significance. It will be a part of what we see when this new order is finally completed by God.

This is where the Gospel touches something deep within us, something that tells us that there really is hope, that what we are doing really is worthwhile in the end, that there really will be a day when everything will be put right.

And it is not a hope in the sense of 'gee I hope it happens'. It is a hope based on historical fact. If we don't believe that, it would ultimately be empty and unfulfilling and wouldn't be real hope.

If God hasn't come to earth in the physical person of Jesus, and if that Jesus wasn't physically resurrected, then nothing really matters. We can make our own meaning and do all we can to bring justice while people are here. But if deep down we still know that it is not everlasting - that in the end everyone still dies and rots in the ground – then there is ultimately no justice, and no hope, and we come back to the sort of philosophy promulgated by Richard Dawkins which says,

'In a universe of blind forces and physical replication, some people are going to get hurt, others are going to get lucky, and you won't find any rhyme or reason in it, nor any justice. The universe we observe has precisely the properties we should expect if there is, at bottom, no design, no purpose, no evil and no good, nothing but blind, pitiless indifference.'

Another Richard, Franciscan priest Richard Rohr, says that the human soul can live without success but it cannot live without meaning. Deep down we all crave significance. We all want to be part of something that matters, something that lasts. Rohr quotes Albert Einstein who said,

'Einstein said at the end, "The only important question is this: Is the universe friendly or not?" Can it all be trusted? Is the final chapter of history victory and resurrection or a dying whimper?'

That is the question we all face. Is there meaning in the universe? Christian faith answers that question with a spectacular and emphatic 'yes!' There is hope and it is real. Goodness really does prevail. As Martin Luther King said in a previous generation, 'The moral arc of the universe is long, and it bends towards justice'.

The message of Scripture is that we live in a friendly universe. And so to the quote above of a Richard Dawkins, we hear the reply from Jesus coming down through the centuries, 'Even the very hairs of your head are all numbered'. You are significant, not just because you might tell yourself that you are, but because you really are.

Good News for the Rich ~ That's Us

Life is interdependent. Nothing you or I ever do is meaningless. Everything has a consequence.

What this means is that the way we live our lives has consequences for those on the other side of the world. There is a direct relationship between our lifestyles and their impact on the planet and the poor.

The Global Footprint Network says that if everyone in the world lived like Australians, we would need five planets to sustain our lifestyle. Our affluent way of life is literally killing us. We can see why Gandhi famously said, when asked what he thought of Western civilisation, 'I think it would be a great idea'.

The prophets of the Old Testament, as well as Jesus, knew about the effects of unjust structures in society. If we only focused on poverty alleviation on its own, the structures that keep people poor would not be changed.

To illustrate this, the story is told of a group of people who decided to watch the movie *Bruce Almighty* in which the main character gets to play God for a day. The group leader asked the group what they would do if they could be God for a day. The main response revolved around redistributing all the wealth in the world so that everyone had an equal amount. It was a fair enough response. But it was quickly pointed out that the next day there would be inequality again, as the structures that made people poor would still be in place. Many such structures keep people in countries like ours rich at the expense of the poor.

We need to work at changing the root causes of poverty. Changing structures is an invaluable part of this, but in the gospels we find that Jesus takes it further. Jesus describes part of his purpose in life as bringing good news to the poor, but as the late Australian scholar Athol Gill said, the Gospel is also good news to the rich. As well as changing structures, it changes people from the inside out.

The story of Zacchaeus in Luke's Gospel is the prime example of this. Zacchaeus was the equivalent of a multi-billionaire mining magnate in Australia today, only more so. Being a tax collector, he was despised by the majority and he ripped people off mercilessly so he could add to his already enormous riches.

So what is Jesus, the friend of the poor, doing inviting himself around for dinner to the house of one of the hated mega-rich who made a living out of exploiting those very people that Jesus set out to befriend? Jesus had a habit of hanging out with the wrong sort of people. He was on about love of God and neighbour and this didn't exclude anyone, even someone as despised as Zacchaeus.

If you read the rest of the story, you will see that Zacchaeus' encounter with Jesus changed everything. He no longer ripped off the poor; he made restitution by paying back four times the amount that he took from people; and his change of heart meant that the local community had financial oppression lifted from them. All because Jesus displayed costly love to someone who everybody else hated.

Fast-forward 2,000 years and compare ourselves to Zacchaeus. In case we may doubt it, we are today's rich. Go to globalrichlist.com, type in your income and see where you fit in terms of your wealth compared to that of everyone else in the world. You might be shocked to find that in this regard we are no different to Zacchaeus.

But the good news that was offered to Zacchaeus is also offered to us. Notice that love and compassion is always at the centre of it; Zacchaeus was never condemned by Jesus. Where the crowds offered hostility, Jesus gave love; where the masses offered condemnation, Jesus offered freedom, and Zacchaeus took up the offer and was a changed man.

Being Christian means offering love regardless of race, gender or class. We have the privilege of being good news to one of the richest nations in the world, of offering transformation that is total and complete: to structures, to society, and to the hearts of rich and poor alike. What a privilege we have.

God is passionately interested in the physical just as much as the spiritual. A creation that is renewed in every way – spiritual, emotional, psychological, and physical – is what God has begun and what we are involved in.

God is a materialist. He loves every part of what he created; physical, spiritual, there is no difference. All is loved by God, and all is being renewed by God. That's why works of justice are important. You and I are part of that renewal, and there is no greater job to do than that.

How to Become More Popular in Three Easy Steps

Ok, be honest. When you saw the title of this article, did you want to read it simply out of curiosity or because you secretly would love to be more popular among your peers?

Well, if you do want to be popular, here's a sure-fire way to have your dream come true. And it has nothing to do with being egotistical. How so, you may ask? Well, read on. Having people come to you in droves will happen if you follow these three easy steps:

1. Don't seek popularity

It is not our aim to simply become popular for its own sake. That's what Jesus' family misunderstood about him. Jesus was never a seeker after fame; it just happened to him. The gospels tell us that the crowds would swarm around him, sometimes so much that he couldn't even move. Such is the need in the world that when we intentionally reach out to hurting and oppressed people, they will come to us.

Popularity, of course, is about wanting to be noticed, wanting to be first. Martin Luther King once gave a sermon on the passage in the gospels where the mother of James and John asks Jesus for her sons to be given the places of prominence in Jesus' new world order.

Jesus then proceeds to tell them what true greatness is. He recognises the natural desire of the human ego to be upfront, to be noticed. King then describes, in the way that only he could in his powerful African-American voice, what Jesus says: 'If you want to be first, well that's great. But to be first you need to serve. If you want to be first, be first at serving, be first at helping others'.

This step is about a collapse of your ego, recognising reality and choosing humility instead. So, don't seek popularity; seek hurting people. They will come to you, guaranteed.

2. Stop reading this and look around you

Go on. Do it. Turn away from where you are right now and look around you. You could bet your life that a good number of the people you can see are dealing with serious personal issues at the moment.

That's it for step 2. That was the easy step. Step 1 is hard because it requires a surrender of your ego. The next and final step is equally hard…

3. Be prepared to suffer

Sooner or later, real love is confronted with sadness and suffering. The price of loving others is often suffering and inconvenience. Jesus knew this firsthand. As the Roman historian, Eusebius, acknowledged 1,700 years ago, you must first count the cost. Here's what he said about Jesus:

'A devoted physician, to save the lives of the sick, sees the horrible danger, yet touches the infected place, and in treating another person's troubles brings suffering on himself.'

Such is the life of one who truly loves. Why would anyone do this? Because it's worth it. It's worth it because you are worth it and because everyone is worth it. To use the words of that wonderful humanitarian and eye surgeon, Fred Hollows, 'Every eye is an eye. When you are doing the surgery there, that is just as important as if you were doing eye surgery on the Prime Minister or King'.

A devotion I read once says that to bring life, Jesus willingly faced death. To offer comfort, he endured suffering. To touch the sorrowing, he shared their sorrow.

Hurting people aren't hard to find. Maybe you are one of them. Widows and orphans, the sick and bereaved, the lonely and neglected, are not only in the majority poor world. They are also in the midst of us. The great news, though, is that Jesus' new order of things is in the midst of us as well.

When we follow Jesus, we seek out hurting people and we find them very easily. Some of the first words in the Gospel of Mark (widely considered to be the oldest gospel) are 'News about him spread quickly over the whole region of Galilee'. People flocked to Jesus because, no matter their background, he accepted them as they were and healed them in every way, allowing them to become full members of society again.

As the above-mentioned devotion goes on to say, let the word get out that you are looking for those who hurt, and you – like Jesus – may find yourself permanently popular! Good news has a way of getting around. When you accept hurting people, word spreads, and you – like Jesus – will never lack an audience.

So there you have it. You want to be popular but at the same time don't want to be full of yourself? Drop the ego, seek out hurting people, and be prepared to suffer. These steps will guarantee you popularity. More importantly, though, they will provide life to a dying world.

Imagine...

For anyone wanting to contribute to making a better world, what they do aligns with their personal dreams for a better world.

When our dreams align with our behaviour, we are more integrated people. It's where the word 'integrity' comes from. When we say a person has integrity, we say that what we see of them is who they really are. There is no mask. As creatures who are inherently relational, our personal transformation becomes part of the transformation of the world as we live out the life of love for which we have been created.

When our dreams and behaviour align with God's dream for us and our world, it is then that we find our true purpose. So let's dream a little. As Bono has said, let's dream out loud:

Imagine living in a world where peace, justice and love are the order of the day; a world where everyone is accepted just for who they are and where there is no fear or mistrust. Then imagine that the ruler of this world had all of these characteristics and more, and actually brought this world into being. Because this is the case, let's call this ruler God.

As you let your imagination take over, you feel a deep longing for this type of world to become a reality, because in your current reality the nature of your fight against poverty means you are faced daily with global injustices, poverty and corruption. But you hear rumours going around that this God longs, just like you, for the whole of existence to be renewed.

Now imagine that this world is not just a far-off hope, but that the building blocks for it have already begun to be put into place. In fact, coming to think of it, you have seen outbreaks of this new world in distant, faraway places, and you have also seen glimpses of it in your own life.

As you ponder a bit more, you feel a spark of excitement in the depth of your being; something has been touched at the very core of who you are as a person. You wonder if working to make this longing a reality is what you were born for.

You soon come across others who share your excitement and passion for this new world. You hear stories of a whole myriad of ways this new world is breaking in. It gradually dawns on you that these outbreaks of this new world are not just happening on their own; they are happening because this God has actually been here in person – the person of Jesus 2000 years ago.

One of the main things that stands out to you as you read more about this Jesus is that he goes on and on about this thing called the 'kingdom of God'. You're not sure what this means so you ask others about it, and they tell you that it is actually this whole new world that you have been seeing outbreaks of in your current life and that it all centres around him.

It then occurs to you that what you have been reading about Jesus shows that every part of his life here was a pointer to this new world. You read elsewhere that he talks about it one day being complete, and calls you to join him in this adventure. You suddenly realise that you have already been on this adventure for a while now, and the excitement within you grows as you recognise that you are part of something bigger than yourself.

As you continue on this new way, you discover that this journey you are on is counter to the prevailing culture, but somehow you know that it matters more than anything else in the world. You are a rebel with a cause. You have found your place. In some unexplainable way you know that you are home with others in God's new community and that every one of your contributions to this new world, matter.

You can now stop imagining, because what you have just read is really taking place. It is not a dream. In the words of C. S. Lewis, 'Aslan is on the move'. God is at work through what you are doing in your efforts to make this world a better place, peeling back the curtain to reveal to the world a bit of what it will be like when everything is made complete.

Jesus and Women

Despite many of the gains made in the last hundred years for women's rights, much remains to be done. Contrary to what is often thought, talking about gender is not just about women; it is also about men.

Rich Stearns' 2009 book, *The Hole in Our Gospel*, reveals some of the devastating statistics that highlight the plight of women around the world. Here are some of them:

- 2/3 of the world's 800 million illiterate are women.
- In Niger, only 15% of the women can read.
- Some 2 million children, mostly girls as young as five years old, are part of the growing commercial sex trade around the world.
- 500 thousand women die every year from complications in childbirth – one every minute.
- Girl babies are even killed in countries where males are considered more valuable. Those who survive are denied property rights and inheritance in many countries.
- Women own less than 1% of the world's property.
- Women work 2/3 of all the world's labour hours but earn only 10% of the world's wages.

As well as this, in countries like India, whose economy has been the topic of news reports for some years now, the plight of women is left unheard. But according to TrustLaw, India is currently the worst place to live in the world if you are a woman.

Bending Towards Justice

It is for these reasons that we find in Jesus the reason that women are to be treated according to their full God-given dignity. The predicament of women in the Middle East during the time of Jesus 2,000 years ago was akin to what we have seen above. For instance,

- most were restricted to roles of little or no authority,
- they were largely confined to their father's or husband's home,
- they were considered to be inferior to men and under the authority of men,
- they were not allowed to testify in court trials,
- they could not go out in public or talk to strangers, and
- when outside of their homes, they were to be doubly veiled.

In this reality, the treatment of women by Jesus was simply revolutionary. When we understand the realities of the culture in which Jesus lived, we can see that he literally put his life in danger by treating women the way he did.

Take the story of the woman at the well in John 4. N. T. Wright says that in that culture many devout Jewish men (remember Jesus was a Jew) would not have allowed themselves to be alone with a woman. If it was unavoidable they certainly wouldn't have started a conversation with her. Also, if you understand the culture of that time you would know that this woman was clearly one of loose morals. She came to the well in the heat of the day when no one else was around, at least no one who knew her and her history. Out of shame she wouldn't want to be seen with other women of the town, nor they with her. Jesus soon reveals that he is well aware of her history, yet he still starts a conversation with her, exposing what she is really looking for in her lifestyle.

There is a saying that goes, 'God loves us just the way we are, but too much to leave us there'. God wants us to grow into people who are more human, people who are able to live out our potential to be the best people we can be. This is exactly what Jesus did with the woman at the well. By speaking with her, he was breaking all the social taboos of the day, and in the process treating her with all the dignity offered to kings and other rulers. And he loved her enough to show her that the way she was going through men was never going to give her what she really wanted.

Another story that illustrates this is that of the woman caught in adultery. This is a wonderful story of how Jesus takes on our pain and suffering. As N. T. Wright says again, the story begins with the religious leaders wanting to stone the woman but ends with them wanting to stone him.

The gospels are full of stories of Jesus' radical treatment of women. They were amongst his closest followers, they were the ones who stayed at the cross when most of his male friends fled the scene, and they were the first at the tomb on the morning of his resurrection (and when they went to tell Jesus' disciples – men – they, of course, didn't believe the women's story).

It is an interesting fact that the portrayal of women in the Gospel stories adds to their authenticity. Most serious biblical scholars say that, given the context of the time, no one would have made up a story about women being treated with such dignity and being portrayed as so central to the story if they weren't true.

The Gospel portrayals of Jesus' death and resurrection highlight this even more strongly. For women to be the ones who stayed at the cross while all the others fled, and women being the first ones who Jesus spoke to after his resurrection, is an outrageous claim... unless it is true.

Jesus Makes an Appearance in the Morning Rush

A story is told of an incredible scene at a busy suburban railway station. A little boy was running a small newsstand where the crowds filed through, all queuing up to touch on their rail cards. Being the morning peak, heaps of people were running down the stairs to the platform to catch the train to avoid being late for work.

As one train was about to leave, a man (who had a job interview to get to) was desperately racing down the stairs, and in his haste plowed right into the little boy. He knocked him off his stool, and the newspapers, magazines and everything else the boy was trying to sell went everywhere.

In a split-second of anxiety, the man stopped, looked at the boy, looked at the train (which he still had time to get to), and looked at the boy again. Then he walked back to the boy, knelt, apologised profusely, and gently helped him up.

After making sure the child was unhurt, the man gathered up the scattered newspapers, sweets, and magazines. Then he took out his wallet and gave the boy twenty dollars. 'Mate', he said, 'I hope this will take care of what was lost or damaged'. As the man got up to get the train, the boy called after him, 'Are you Jesus?'.*

One of the many attractive characteristics of Jesus is that he never saw anything as an interruption to what he was doing. There are many cases in the Gospels where he is on his way somewhere and is stopped in his tracks by someone. In none of these instances does Jesus say, 'Look, I'm busy at the moment, can you come back in half an hour?'. He is instead unhurried, filled with compassion and ready to respond.

It seems that, although he did so much that John's Gospel says the whole world couldn't contain all the books that would be written, Jesus never felt rushed for time. He was driven by love.

Jesus has never been more relevant to our lives than he is today. He, of all people, knew what it was to be in great demand everywhere he went. How many times are we told in the Gospels that crowds pressed in on him from every side, that there were thousands of people following him? Yet not once does he come across as being rushed or stressed about all the things he had to do in the course of his day. How did he cope?

While I believe that Jesus was God, I also realise he was human just like me. He lived in twenty-four hour days. He ate, he slept and he went about his daily business. Jesus, though, lived by the attitude of surrender to what was right rather than what he felt like doing. And therein lies the answer for us.

Asking God each day for his will to be done in our lives, come what may, allows us to live with minimal stress. There is always time to do God's will. Peace lies in choosing to do the right thing in any given moment, not the thing that will necessarily save the most time or the thing we really feel like doing.

It is still possible to live a relaxed and peaceful life in the 21st century. We can draw great encouragement from St Paul's letter to the Romans where he exhorts us not to be conformed to the pattern of this world but to be transformed by the renewing of our minds. The pattern of this world in the 21st century is to have it all and have it now. But study after study has shown that this simply does not work. Never has and never will.

Bending Towards Justice

In our desperate quest to fit more and more into our lives, to experience more and to have more, the 'more' that we are being left with is depression that is ten times as high as it was at the end of the Second World War, and a constant restlessness that our lives are just too busy.

The man at the train station showed that we don't have to be slaves to time. There is nothing that can get in the way of us choosing to follow Jesus. Nothing. Allowing him to transform us by the renewing of our minds, the renewing of our attitudes and the renewing of our sense of time gives us the freedom that all our time-saving techniques are really looking for.

*The story above is fictional, but based on a true occurrence many years ago.

Jesus of Australia

There is a famous *Farside* cartoon from Gary Larson's brilliant series that shows God sitting at a computer screen up in heaven. On the screen is some ordinary bloke walking down the street. Right above him is a crane carrying a large piano that dangles over his head. At this moment, the cartoon shows God with his finger over the 'Smite' button on the keyboard, ready to crush the poor, innocent man.

This is the image that many people have of God, if thoughts of the Almighty ever come to mind. God is up there in heaven, a sadistic, smug look on his (male) face, ready to smack us over the head just because he can.

Unfortunately, this view of God is a view that has been affirmed by many Christians over many years. Australian history since European settlement has often promulgated a view of a God who is angry and ready to punish, rather than the Jesus of the Gospels, who is a God full of love, grace and forgiveness.

Over the last two hundred years, the Australian psyche has generally reflected a sense of rebellion towards authority. This has come largely from our convict heritage where our first settlements outside those of our indigenous brothers and sisters were formed on the backs of people who had been sent here against their will. It was overwhelmingly poor people who had committed petty crimes who set up Australia as we have known it since 1788.

As with much in prison systems around the world (and certainly still in Australia), prisoners – in this case convicts – were there to be punished. They were scum and were to be treated as such, rather than being rehabilitated so as to minimise their chances of reoffending once free, thus providing them and their fellow citizens a chance at a more peaceful life.

Adding to the problem was that the church of the time generally went along for the ride, proclaiming a God of judgment, there to punish people like convicts who had done the wrong thing. Samuel Marsden, the 'Flogging Parson', was an extreme example of a Minister not only preaching but in his case administering gruesome punishment to these 'sinners'.

It is no wonder, then, that Australian history since European settlement has shown a disdain for things religious and has not wanted a whole lot to do with God. As a result of our European history, we have had built into us a certain lack of respect for authority. We have idolised people and events that portray our underdog status, even if some events have been catastrophic failures. Events like Gallipoli are heroic to us because they portray selfless courage and sacrifice; Ned Kelly is a hero to many despite being a murderer, because he is seen as standing up against the establishment. The Eureka Stockade is still commemorated every year in Ballarat as a celebration of the rights of the oppressed. Don Bradman and Phar Lap are celebrated as Australians who took on the world and won.

The beautiful irony of this disdain for authority, including things religious, is that Australians – generally without realising it – have developed a genuine affinity with the Jesus of the gospels. Jesus fits very well into the Australian psyche. He was an underdog from the beginning, born at the back of an inn in an animals' trough, and hanging out at pubs with the wrong crowd, with just the sort of 'sinners' that our convict ancestors were. He was even known as the 'friend of sinners' and was accused of being a drunkard and a glutton. Not what you might expect from the Son of God.

Jesus also stood up against the establishment, calling out pretence for what it was, one time even making a whip out of cords and ripping into the equivalent of bankers in the temple. Linked to that, like a good Aussie, he couldn't stand hypocrisy. He suffered at the hands of the authorities, treated unjustly even unto death, a death of the most brutal kind imaginable in those days, a Roman crucifixion. An innocent man silenced by hypocrisy and oppression.

Whatever people's ideas about Jesus, a common belief is that they generally don't find anything wrong with him. There is something about him that is respected, even revered. We would do well to go back to the gospels and see for ourselves the relevance of Jesus to Australians.

There is one area though where Australians have never had a real sense of connection to Jesus. It is the area that is central to his earthly existence: his resurrection from the dead. Our rampant materialism and resultant high rates of depression, loneliness and addiction are a symptom of an ultimate loss of hope. It is hope though that marks the Christian faith. Ultimate, eternal, existential hope.

At its core, the very essence of Christian faith is hope. It is the ultimate good news, often seeming to be too good to be true for a cynical people like us who have not known ultimate hope.

Christian faith proclaims a God who is love personified. It proclaims a God who has come down to Earth to be with us in our suffering, to show us how to live within it, and ultimately to lead us out of it into a new day that has already dawned.

When the sun rises each morning, it can remind us that the other Son has also risen. The sun brings us out of a darkened night, the other Son brings light to a darkened world. The resurrection is nothing less than the greatest news in history. It is the Son rising in splendour, showing us what a new world can be like, what a new world *will* be like.

The gospels show Australians a Jesus they can relate to, the Jesus of the underdog, the Jesus of the oppressed, the Jesus who hangs out with the ones that others call losers. Thank God for a Jesus who knows us Australians more intimately than we know ourselves.

Living the dream

In the last few years, the term 'living the dream' has become more common when we greet each other. It is supposed to mean that we are living the life we want to live. It can be a good sign when people say that. If nothing else, it means that people are to some extent satisfied with their lives.

The great Australian dream has for years been to own your own home, something which is now out of reach for more and more people. But what if we could align our dreams to a bigger dream, the dream of God for the world? What if we could live the dream of a world where there are no more tears and no more pain, as the last book in the Bible, Revelation, tells us? And what if, as author Scot McKnight says, that dream could transform us at the very core of who we are?

When our dreams align with God's dream, we start to come alive. Another author, John Eldredge, says he laments the fact that so many go along with dreams that help them in making a living but deny them making a life. He says, 'Don't ask yourself what the world needs. Ask yourself what makes you come alive, because what the world needs is people who have come alive'.

McKnight goes on to say that, 'At the core of every dream you have, behind every dream you have, ahead of every dream others have, and in the centre of every good dream every human has, we will find the kingdom dream of Jesus'.

We are hardwired to live this dream. If you look at the great social movements, you can see that history belongs to the dreamers. There is much bad news in the world today. Every day, we see news of the demonisation of asylum seekers, the ugliness of terrorism, the epidemic of domestic violence, and rates of depression and loneliness that belie the image of a wonderful society in the richest country in the world. But continue to persevere we do, and dream on we must.

It is those who dare to dream who are the shakers and movers of history. William Wilberforce's dream of an end to slavery was seen as hopelessly utopian at the time, as slavery was the very foundation of the might of the British Empire. But year after year he persisted and in the end justice prevailed. When Martin Luther King spoke of his dream of little black children and little white children holding hands together, his dream was also seen as hopelessly utopian, yet Barack Obama was elected the first black President in the history of the United States. When Nelson Mandela was languishing in a South African prison for twenty-seven years, his dream of an end to apartheid was seen as hopelessly out of reach, yet he became President of his country and became a hero to millions.

History belongs to the dreamers. God's Spirit within empowers, inspires and motivates us to go on when setbacks would throw us off guard.

In talking about God's dream, Jesus used kingdom language because it was appropriate for his time, but it is still helpful for us today because it presupposes that there is a king. In our lives as believers, the dream we are aiming for is not a kingdom without a king, but a kingdom with the characteristics of the King. All throughout the Scriptures we are told that God is a God of love and justice, is a wonderful counsellor and Prince of Peace. Imagine what a world with such characteristics would be like.

Living the dream of God transforms the world and in the process transforms us. Despite setbacks, one day our dream will come true, and we will know that it has all been worth it.

Love and the Facebook Hug Vest

Some years ago, some students at MIT in the United States developed a bodywarmer type vest that translates every Facebook 'like' you receive into an actual hug. Bizarre I know, but it says a lot more about the human condition than we may care to realise.

There was a study in *The Atlantic magazine*, also a few years back, which said that social media such as Facebook, Twitter and the like are actually making us lonelier, despite us being more connected than at any previous time in human history. The article says that, 'What Facebook has revealed about human nature – and this is not a minor revelation – is that a connection is not the same thing as a bond, and that instant and total connection is no salvation, no ticket to a happier, better world or a more liberated version of humanity'.

Are we saying that social media is bad? No, just that we need to keep it in its proper place and remain realistic about what it can and can't do.

What does a device that gives you a physical hug from a virtual 'like' say about our culture? And what does it say about that most fundamental of human needs: love? Since time immemorial, humanity has pondered the question, 'what is love?'.

Love is one of those things we never fully get a handle on, but one thing we can be sure of is that love is relational. A virtual Facebook hug can never replace human contact, which is why, if we rely on these things to make us feel connected, they will actually have the opposite effect of making us more empty than before.

Real love is fascinating; there is always something new to learn about it. That's why it's worth giving our lives to it. Until the day we die, there is always more to learn about how we can be more loving. But what actually is love?

One of the best descriptions of a personal love comes from C.S. Lewis' *The Lion, the Witch and the Wardrobe*, in which young Lucy is finding out from one of Narnia's wonderful creatures about Aslan, the God/Christ character. Upon hearing about Aslan for the first time, Lucy asks if he is safe (being a lion and all). She is told in no uncertain terms, 'Safe?! 'Course he's not safe. But he's good!' Eugene Petersen, author of *The Message* translation of the Bible, has a similarly profound definition. Writing of the fact that love is the very character of God, Petersen says, 'God is kind but he's not soft'.

Many of us wouldn't think of love in these terms. Love is not a warm fuzzy feeling; it is an act of the will. Love acts despite how we feel. Contrary to what many us may have been taught to believe, love is like steel; it is not weak. Love is ferocious; it never flinches; it is tough and is never walked over. And in the words of the sequel to the magnificent *Phantom of the Opera*, love never dies.

For millions of Christians, their favourite Bible verse is John 3:16 – 'For God so loved the world that he gave his only Son, that whoever believes in him would not perish but have eternal life'. But how many Christians could recite off the top of their heads 1 John 3:16 (and 17). Look it up. That is what the Gospel is about. It is love in action.

This is why passages like 1 John 3:16-17 are so close to the heart of God. The heart of God is a heart that suffers. As U2 sing, 'a heart that hurts is a heart that beats'. A heart that is able to feel the deep suffering of the world is a heart that is alive.

When Jesus was in the Garden of Gethsemane on the eve of his crucifixion, he said to his best friends a number of times that he was distressed to the point of death. That's what love does. Love means taking on a willingness to suffer, because the one who loves knows that the cause of love is what will win in the end.

This is why many people of faith around the world choose to suffer. Some of you reading this know this all too well. You have suffered because of your faith, and it is that very faith that gives you courage beyond yourselves.

These are the real heroes of our time. These are the ones who go into the places of heartbreak around the world, the places of war, the places of hate, the places of injustice, the places where the smell is worse than a sewer in the slums where people try to eke out a daily existence. They go into the places where the losers are, where the nobodies are, and they hang out there. And they do it because that's exactly where Jesus would hang out.

Love will not stand by and watch evil get its way. But the methods of love are so different to what we think is common sense. Love, though, is not about common sense. This is why we need outside help to empower us to embody God's love in the world.

Embodying this love is so difficult that we cannot do it alone. Embodying this love is also personal. But it is not just personal; it is a Person, a Person living in us. Jesus is love personified. He is a real person we can relate with and seek guidance from to do it his way.

If we are committed to this Love, we will see that it constantly disarms us. This is what is thrilling about following Jesus. It is never boring; there is always something over the next hill, and it will most often surprise us. It will show us things like the fact that love is not 'nice' but giving; it is not passive-aggressive but brutally honest; and it is not timid but forcefully assertive.

Stacked up against this somewhat disturbing picture of love, we have to ask ourselves whether or not we are Christian. It is a healthy question to ask. It was Socrates four hundred years before Jesus who said that the unexamined life is not worth living.

Being Christian requires us to ask the courageous questions: are we buying into the story of the prevailing culture where our ultimate aim is to make money? Or are we seeking to follow Jesus into the difficult places and do what is right come what may, whether that means we make our millions or not? These are the questions any Christian needs to ask themselves. Easy and wide is the road that leads to downfall, and many follow it. But narrow and uphill is the road that leads to life, and there are few who follow it. These are the words of Jesus, and they are words that challenge us and spur us on.

Love is what every human heart needs. It is tough, it is challenging, and it is life. Love is the heartbeat of our identity. May our prayer this day be that God help us to know this Love and make it known throughout a broken world.

Love in all its Fullness

If I give everything I own to the poor and even go to the stake to be burned as a martyr, but I don't love, I've gotten nowhere.

(1 Corinthians 13:3)

As a Christian, my view of the best way to work for the creation of a better world includes a word that you wouldn't normally associate with the alleviation of poverty and the seeking of justice. That word is 'love'.

The love of God underlies everything in the Christian Gospel and is the foundation of my identity.

A Christian approach to justice is ultimately rooted in love. It is love that is transformational, that brings structural change to societies as well as personal change to human hearts. Love is all-encompassing. That's why St Paul talks so strongly about it in 1 Corinthians 13. This is the passage we hear most often at weddings, but St Paul is applying it to all of life.

Scot McKnight, an American theologian, surely had 1 Corinthians 13 in mind when he wrote about the relationship between justice and love: 'The fundamental Christian ethic is love, not justice. Justice is a manifestation of love. So, in discussions of justice, if it is not anchored in love... then justice becomes too closely connected to laws and constitutions and secularized theories of rights. Justice in the Bible is moral behaviour that conforms to the will of God... and... when justice runs its course it becomes love'.

The ultimate goal of my life is to see the reign of love in the world. This love is rooted in the very character of God – God is love. Love seeks the transformation of the whole creation. This is why seeking justice on its own, in the sense of alleviating poverty and changing structures, is not enough. If I focus my efforts only on the alleviation of poverty and the changing of unjust structures, real change will not take place. The human heart needs changing too, otherwise the mistakes of the past are doomed to be repeated.

Michael Edwards, Director of the Ford Foundation's Governance and Civil Society Program, has spent more than twenty years researching organisations that work for peace and social justice. As a result of his work, he has become convinced there is 'a missing link in many of these efforts that holds back their effectiveness and achievement, and this missing link is love, or more precisely the failure to use love as the basis for the functioning of the organisation and its work'.

In his reflections on the connections between spirituality and social transformation, Edwards draws inspiration from the example of Martin Luther King, and concludes that, 'marrying a rich inner life dedicated to the cultivation of loving kindness and compassion with the practice of new forms of politics, economics and public policy is… the key to social transformation'.

Love is the key to social transformation. As Christians, the source of our identity is rooted in love.

The love of God transforms everything. It transforms an Indian woman who believes that the reason she is poor is because she was born into the wrong caste. It tells her that she is a loved child of God no matter what caste she was born into. Love transforms a Tanzanian man who experiences fear when he hears rain on the roof because he believes the gods are upset with him. It tells him that there is no fear in love, that perfect love drives out all fear.

Research carried out by the World Bank shows that poor people define poverty primarily as a lack of identity. Love transforms that, both in the people we relate with and in ourselves. Letting the all-encompassing love of God infuse everything we are is the key to our lives. Through love we find life in all its fullness.

Reverend Billy and the Church of Stop Shopping

Have you heard of the movie, *What Would Jesus Buy?* It's a brilliant spoof of all that Christmas has become for millions of people trapped in the shopping frenzy that is the silly season.

The film follows Reverend Billy and his Church of Stop Shopping Gospel Choir travelling throughout the United States as they try to help consumers open their eyes to the madness that they are participating in every December.

One of the most poignant scenes in the movie is when the choir would roll up to the front door of some unsuspecting family and start singing Christmas carols. 'How nice' you might say, until you heard the brilliantly farcical take on some well-known lyrics. Take their version of *Joy to the World:*

Joy to the World!
In the Form of Goods!
Consume! Consume! Consume!
Bright Plastics This and That's!
For Screaming Little Brats!
Take the SUV to the Mall
Take the SUV to the Mall.

The unfortunate truth is that these words are a more accurate description of Christmas for most Australians than the traditional lyrics of this beautiful carol.

It's sad that it takes a fake minister to bring across a message that Jesus would surely endorse were he here in person. Reverend

Billy and his Church of Stop Shopping Gospel Choir sure get the message across that we have done something terrible to that wonderful time of year when it is all about clamouring all over the person in front of you to get that special bargain.

What Would Jesus Buy? shows how far we have digressed from not only what Christmas is all about, but even from the origins of Santa Claus, formerly known as Saint Nicholas. This great saint, a young man raised by Christian parents in the 3rd century in what is now Turkey, was known for taking literally Jesus' words to 'sell all you have and give the money to the poor'. It is documented that 'Nicholas used his whole inheritance to assist the needy, the sick, and the suffering. He dedicated his life to serving God and was made Bishop of Myra while still a young man. Bishop Nicholas became known throughout the land for his generosity to those in need, his love for children'.

Quite a contrast to the jolly red man we see at Christmas time every year. Many centuries later, the memory of Saint Nicholas and his beautiful spirit is as unfamiliar as snow in an Australian summer. The fact is that many parents in this country now dread Christmas because of the stress it creates in terms of what on earth to buy the kids this year.

What this shows us again is how counter-cultural is the story of the God who came as a babe in a manger, relegated to a smelly stable out the back because there was no room for his parents at the inn. At Christmas, we celebrate a God who came as a person, a God who made the ultimate sacrifice to involve himself in the poverty and oppression of what is life for much of this planet's population.

Christmas for so many is a painful time; for many others it is a joyful time, and for others still it is a time of stress they could well do without. If it is a painful time for you, then remember the

One who came to stand beside you in your pain, the One who understands what it is to be rejected, to have nothing, and to be told he doesn't belong in his own neighbourhood.

If Christmas is a joyful time for you, then thank the One who gave all he had to come and eat at table with us, to offer us grace upon grace, even when, no, especially when, that is the very thing we do not deserve.

And if you can't wait for Christmas to be over so you can relax, then allow yourself to be set free by giving of yourself this Christmas, especially to those for whom Christmas is painful. May your gift be in the form of love and community, and gifts that have meaning. Your gifts may be in the form of a goat or literacy skills through the gift catalogues that many NGOs offer. The options are endless, and you may just find that you are giving to Jesus himself.

As the next Christmas comes around, may it be a meaningful one for you, filled with the Spirit of the Christ who gives to all without measure.

Sharing Fruit to End Poverty

An anthropologist was studying the habits of some people in Africa. He proposed a game for the children. He put a basket full of fruits near a tree and told them that whoever got there first won the fruits. What happened next though just blew his mind.

When he told them to run, they all took each other's hands and ran together, then sat down as one, enjoying their treats. When the anthropologist asked them why they had run like that, as one of them could have had all the fruits for himself, they said, 'How can one of us be happy if all the others are sad?'

That day, the children showed the anthropologist a glimpse of what it means to be fully alive.

If someone asked you what poverty is, what would you say? The first thing many of us would think of would be that it involves a lack of money and food. And perhaps you would say it is a lack of access to many of the things that most of us take for granted, like a place to work and clean water. You would be correct in that assumption. But what if you asked a person living in poverty the same question? What would they say?

In 1999, the World Bank carried out a major survey of 60,000 people living in poverty around the world. Called *Voices of the Poor*, the survey asked them how they defined poverty. The overwhelming response was that, while poverty definitely involves a lack of access to goods and services, it is fundamentally about a lack of identity – knowing who we are and being confident of our importance and value in the world. One respondent from Jamaica said, 'Poverty is like living in jail, living under bondage, waiting to be free'.

People living in poor communities typically feel ignored. They say that they are not seen or heard. They feel 'less than' those that have more than they do. They feel powerless to be able to change their circumstances, shamed and humiliated.

Loss of identity inevitably impacts people's relationships. It impacts the farming family where the father is forced to go into the city to earn money. His children are deprived of security and a male role model. It impacts millions of children whose parents have died of AIDS, children who are now forced to look after one another, taking on the role of parent, bread-winner and caretaker. The loss of important relationships, such as a parent, severely affects the type of people these children will become later in life.

Relationship lies at the very heart of our identity as humans. It is impossible to think of who we are apart from our connections with others. Our psychological wellbeing and our spirituality depend on the quality of our relationships. Spirituality is as natural as breathing for most people in the world. In fact the origin of the term 'spirituality' means to be fully alive.

Lifting people out of poverty involves lifting people into positive and healthy relationships and a sense of identity. It is allowing people to live to their full potential, emotionally, spiritually and materially. It allows them to walk tall in the knowledge of their inherent, God-given worth.

Our relationships are what define us as humans. Thinking of others and caring for others fosters what we need as humans to be fully alive – mental wellbeing, spiritual connection and having our needs met. It is about having life in all its fullness. That's what we look forward to.

As St Irenaeus said, 'The glory of God is a human being fully alive'. When humanity is fully alive, that will be the end of poverty. Now who wants to share some fruit?

Sport as a Reflection of the Dream of God

The Olympic Games seem to be the one event in the world where nations come together for a short time to celebrate a common cause – the cause of sport.

For us in Australia, it is that time once every four years when we get blanket media coverage of every event that contains an Aussie, and when many of us turn up to work bleary-eyed having been up in the wee hours watching our heroes do their thing for their country.

Sport is part of the fabric of this country. It has been since Don Bradman and Phar Lap brought such hope into the hopelessness of Australians battling through the Depression years of the 1930s. We have watched through tear-stained eyes as Australia took the America's Cup from the Americans in 1983 after 132 years, when Cathy Freeman won gold in Sydney in 2000, and we celebrated for days after John Aloisi put Australia into the 2006 soccer World Cup after years of disappointment. We pretty much punch above our weight when it comes to our sporting achievements in this country.

But we are, of course, not the only nation who loves our sport. In South America, soccer is almost a religion. It is not much different in England, where the mood of supporters is reflected in the weekly fortunes of their favourite club. The seriousness with which they take their football was epitomised by former Liverpool manager, Bill Shankly, who once famously remarked, 'Football isn't a matter of life and death; it's much more important than that!'

Bending Towards Justice

Sport has an amazing capacity to bring the world together, and the Olympics, of all global sporting events, are perhaps the best example of this. For two weeks every four years, most of the world watches as occasionally, nations which have been at war with each other are able to come together in a sporting contest and display a spirit of friendship that puts their political leaders to shame.

Unfortunately, over the years, the professionalisation of sport has taken some of the soul out of it. But in communities all over the world, children can be seen playing soccer out of a ball made of the most basic materials. In India, millions of children play cricket in the laneways and byways of that vast land. And events such as the Paralympics demonstrate that anyone of whatever ability can participate.

The idea that participation is open to anyone is a wonderful analogy for the kingdom of God. Jesus talks in Luke's Gospel of the great banquet to which everyone is invited, regardless of status.

Similarly, sport should be a celebration. This can be seen in places like Senegal where they celebrate the end of harvest season by having wrestling matches to which the whole community comes along. And on nearby Gorree island, the children play soccer in front of hundreds of people from the local community. When someone scores a goal, everyone runs onto the ground and celebrates. In Senegal, they see sport as a God-given gift.

Everyone has certain gifts, and to watch someone with a sporting gift is a sight to behold. We can see the beauty of God's creation when we watch someone like Roger Federer play tennis, or the sublime technical perfection of a Sachin Tendulkar drive through the covers for four at the MCG. It is poetry in motion, beautiful to watch.

This is perhaps most famously seen in the life of Eric Liddell, whose life and achievements are shown in the movie *Chariots of Fire*. Liddell was a committed Christian and saw his running ability as a chance to glorify God. When asked how his running was related to his faith, he replied, 'When I run I feel God's pleasure'.

Gifting or not, sport offers a chance to celebrate for poor communities around the world. Just as in Senegal, children in Rwanda play soccer with a ball made out of plastic bags tied together. They see playing soccer as a chance to get out of the shackles of poverty. In indigenous communities in Australia, it is the same. Ask any young indigenous boy what they want to do when they grow up and they all say they want to play AFL.

Sport provides hope for millions of children the world over, and when played in the right spirit, everyone walks away a winner. Gordon Preece of the Evangelical Alliance remarks that we can view sport as 'a part of God's good creation and even a glimpse of a new, perfect, playful world'. And Marcus Curnow, from Newmarket Baptist Church, says that sport is 'an opportunity to reconcile differences or experience a sense of belonging that some have rarely known'.

Perhaps the most wonderful piece of sportsmanship in Australian history was the gesture of John Landy running a mile race in 1956 and going back to help opponent Ron Clarke who had fallen over. Marcus Curnow goes on to say that, 'In an increasingly disconnected...world where we often passively consume highlight packages of the "unbelievable" feats of a sporting elite... such characters and moments bear witness to the value of the ordinary and the believable'.

We see the life of Jesus mimicked in gestures such as John Landy's. They are gestures that bring out the good in us, the good that we all, deep down, long to be like. Landy's incredible gesture reflected the Olympic Charter whose goal is to 'place sport at the service of the harmonious development of humankind, with a view to promoting a peaceful society concerned with the preservation of human dignity'. This, of course, is exactly along the lines of what Jesus is on about. In fact, when Baron Pierre de Coubertin, the father of the modern Olympics, made his famous statement in 1908 that, 'The importance of these Olympiads is not so much to win as to take part... The important thing in life is not the triumph but the struggle. The essential thing is not to have won but to have fought well', words that have become the Olympic Creed, he was inspired in his thinking by a sermon at St Paul's Cathedral by the Bishop of Central Pennsylvania.

The Olympics are a reflection of the renewed creation that we all long for, as the embodiment of what is possible when we live as we are designed to.

Stand for Something or Fall for Anything

Alleviating poverty is one thing, but asking why those same people are poor is not a popular question to ask.

One crucial aspect of alleviating poverty involves advocacy. We can't have a lasting impact on poverty without it. If we don't deal with the root causes of poverty, which are overwhelmingly to do with injustice, any work to alleviate poverty will be in vain.

Advocacy is about speaking truth to power. This inevitably involves swimming against the tide of popular opinion. When we take a stand for what is right, when we stand up for love and justice in the world, we inevitably come up against conflict. And some people will always be upset. That's the way it works when you unsettle the status quo.

Jesus knew all about that. Contrary to what is spoken in many churches, Jesus was not a nice guy – far from it. Nice guys didn't get themselves crucified by the Romans. Jesus was both a threat to the might of Rome and a threat to the Church of his day. And we, in doing his work, are to be the same. As author Dan Allender has said, Jesus said we would be known by our love, not by our manners.

Jesus was also unequivocally political. If you read the gospels in context, they are clear as day about that. That's why, as followers of Jesus, we work to do all we can to bring lasting change for the majority of the world's population. Wise people have said over the years that a civilisation is measured by how it treats its most vulnerable citizens.

Enabling and empowering people to 'speak truth to power' is part of the process of helping to create a new society, with new values and new ideals. We don't want a society where we are told that the economy is the most important thing that matters, where we are told it is all about us and how much we can line our pockets with. The message we have is written on our hearts. The Spirit is at work, changing us and changing the world through us.

As long as we are doing what is right, we will come up against some sort of resistance. The great paradox of this is that the way of struggle is the way to happiness. Jesus said the road to life is narrow and uphill. That goes completely against everything that is ingrained into us. So much so that there are few Christians that really live by it. It really is the road less travelled. If you follow it, people will tell you that you are odd.

Proverbs 29:18 says 'without a vision the people perish'. Humanity needs a standard to live by. If we don't have that we are lost; the blind leading the blind. That's why the saying 'if you don't stand for something, you'll fall for anything' is so profound.

Christian faith says there are moral absolutes in the universe. Deep down, each of us has this moral law in our hearts. As we come closer to the heart of God, we are able to determine more clearly what is right and what is evil. We need power greater than our own to guide us in what is right, and to give us the courage to live it out, come what may. May God give us strength to continue to do so.

Successful Social Movements

In 1930, a bright young German theological student deemed too young to be ordained decided to travel to the United States to pursue post-graduate studies. There, he made friends with another student – who invited him along to his church in Harlem.

Worshipping with the African American congregation, the 24-year-old German began to see things 'from below' – from the perspective of those who suffer oppression.

This encounter led to his personal conversion – from being a theologian focused on the intellectual side of Christianity, to being a dedicated man of faith, resolved to carry out the teachings of Jesus.

That young man was Dietrich Bonhoeffer.

A pastor and theologian of great intellect, he went on to repeatedly speak out against Hitler's persecution of Jews, declaring that the church must not simply 'bandage the victims under the wheel, but jam the spoke in the wheel itself'.

Despite persecution, Bonhoeffer insisted that Christ, not the Führer, was the head of the Church. His involvement in the attempted assassination of Hitler led to his arrest and eventual execution.

Empowered by God, Christians like Bonhoeffer have become a shining light in a world of sin, by speaking up and starting social movements that have brought injustice to an end.

Think of some of the most successful social movements in history: Martin Luther King and the civil rights movement in the United States; Nelson Mandela and Desmond Tutu and the anti-apartheid movement in South Africa; Gandhi and the independence movement in India; Oscar Romero in El Salvador; William Wilberforce and the abolitionist movement – the list goes on.

These movements all had a spiritual base. More specifically, they had Christian faith at the centre of them. Even Gandhi, who wasn't a Christian, based much of his non-violence on the Sermon on the Mount. He said it was the greatest teaching that has ever been given.

Why are social movements with a strong Christian foundation so successful? For a start, they go beyond just protesting. They offer an alternative, one that puts human dignity at the forefront. It is the kingdom of God alternative.

Working for the kingdom of God involves transformation of every part of human existence. This includes of course the human heart which Jeremiah describes as deceitful above all things (Jeremiah 17:9).

History shows that the early Christians brought about major changes in the Roman Empire during the first few centuries after Christ. Social historian Rodney Stark explains that the explosive growth of the Christian movement was caused primarily by their acts of service and unconditional love to the outcast people of their day.

Acts 2 and 4 describe how the new Christian community lived out their lives, and the impact they had on those around them.

They were a beacon of love and hope in the midst of what was a dark and miserable existence for thousands of people. At a time when women and girls were second-class citizens, the Christians showed them their true dignity as equals. As outcasts such as lepers were left to die, the Christians took them in and cared for them.

The impact of the early Christians was such that by the time Constantine became the emperor in the 4th century, half the population of the Roman Empire was Christian.

In a world marred by sin, these faithful followers of Jesus saw the outworking of their faith as the solution to the problems of the world. They gave their lives to help bring in the kingdom that Jesus began. Their faith was inseparably intertwined with their actions.

Today, Christians are still called to be a beacon of hope for those facing injustice.

Like Dietrich Bonhoeffer all those years ago, let's speak out fearlessly against injustice and shine the light of Christ's goodness into a world of darkness.

The Best is Yet to Come

In his book, *The Road Less Travelled*, M. Scott Peck begins with the opening line, 'Life is difficult'. It is something we all know. It doesn't take much insight to realise that there is a whole lot of suffering in the world. Every single person experiences suffering of some sort throughout their life. For some it is more acute than others, but no one escapes. Suffering is a part of life.

The letter of James in the New Testament opens with what looks like the quite bizarre encouragement to 'consider it pure joy... whenever you face trials of many kinds'. Hardly the kind of 'encouragement' that most of us would consider to be helpful and edifying. Why on earth would it be 'pure joy' facing difficulties in your life? Does James have any idea about suffering?

As with any historical document, we need to look at this in context. It has often been said that a text taken out of context is a pretext; or, as Jarrod McKenna has put it, a text taken out of context is a sure sign you're being conned! So what is the context in which James' letter was written? Well, he was writing to a group of Christians who, through persecution, had been scattered all over their area of the world. They, and James himself (who was later executed for his faith), knew firsthand what suffering was.

It is pertinent to note too that James does not mention anything about being happy. He talks instead about joy. There is a big difference. Pastoral carer Rowland Croucher says that joy is what is left over after all the things that bring external happiness are gone. Happiness is when things in our life work out, but joy is not dependent on external circumstances.

The best example I know of about joy in difficult circumstances is that of Jesus himself on the night of what we call the Last Supper. The only time in all the gospels that Jesus talks about his own joy is on this fateful and tragic night. Consider what was going on when he told the disciples of his joy. He knows he is about to die, it is *after* he is betrayed by one of his best friends, and he knows that all of his other closest friends will desert him, and that one of them, Peter, will deny that he even knows him.

During all this, his time of greatest need, Jesus knew joy. That doesn't mean he put on a smiley face and thought 'isn't life wonderful?' It means that he faced his pain, fully felt it, agonised over it, but didn't let it get the better of him. He knew that whatever his circumstances, God was with him. He was secure, and nothing could take that away from him.

The Christian psychologist, Larry Crabb, says that disappointment in life can drive us to hope, the hope that there will come a better day, when the kingdom of God, the new society of God, will be a reality. That is what brings us joy. That our current travails will one day end. Hope is alive, hope abounds. And with it, joy.

This is where we have much to learn from the majority poor world. There is often a sense of joy and contentment that is seen in people living in poverty. Now this observation of the contentment of the poor is, of course, a gross generalisation; there will be many poor who are not happy. Poverty does that. It strips dignity and identity from those under its curse. But the point remains that it is those living in poverty who generally live a more carefree life, and, conversely it is the well-to-do who live with the greatest anxiety over keeping their lifestyles secure.

Many of us are, or have been, experiencing pain in our personal lives, and most of us would feel the pain of seeing others suffer throughout the world. Out of this, let James speak to us again. Continuing on from the verse above about considering it pure joy when we face all kinds of trials, he says that 'the testing of your faith produces perseverance. Let perseverance finish its work so that you may be mature and complete, not lacking anything'.

It is not just James, but the whole of the New Testament that has a theme of suffering running through it. St Paul says that the suffering we experience now is nothing compared to the coming good times, when the reign of God, of justice, peace and transformation will be complete.

Joy comes when we learn to accept life on life's terms. We see this in the eyes of the many children living in destitute conditions around the world. We see it in the maturity of someone like Martin Luther King, who talked about redemptive suffering, which he described as 'a willingness to accept suffering without seeking revenge or retribution'.

It is the Spirit of God that empowers us to keep going when suffering occurs, whether in our own lives or in the lives of others with whom we are working. The joy of service is real when we allow God to reign in our own lives, take our eyes off ourselves and keep our eyes on the prize, the greater good, the good for which we are all made.

I love the attitude of Martin Luther King when, on the night before he died, he gave perhaps his most moving speech. He spoke of the future of the civil rights movement, but he could have been speaking about what many people are or have been going through. He said, 'We've got some difficult days ahead. But it really doesn't matter... now... I'm not concerned about that now. I just want to do God's will'. What maturity! That is the example of Jesus, that come what may, we do the will of God, his good, pleasing and perfect will!

The Disarming Beauty of Grace

Some years ago, the cyclist Lance Armstrong was exposed as a drug cheat. What most of the media missed reporting was the fact that the Armstrong scandal highlighted our own judgments when we see someone else fall from grace. Former Melbourne City Councillor David Wilson wrote at the time about the fact that how we perceive Lance Armstrong's failings tells us a lot about ourselves.

Wilson made the point that before we say what a fraud Armstrong was, we need to remember that there is good and bad in all of us. The fact is that if we were to expect God to get rid of all evil in the world, he would have to destroy every single one of us, because, as Alexander Solzhenitsyn said, the line between good and evil runs right through the middle of every human heart. No one is all evil and no one is all good. As Wilson went on to say, 'This reminder should keep the judgment dogs at bay and the appreciation of grace and forgiveness uppermost in our minds, without condoning what Armstrong has done'.

What is this thing Christians call 'grace'? It is a word that is bandied about a fair bit. Above, we referred to Lance Armstrong's 'fall from grace'. We might also talk about a dancer who moves gracefully; or someone might be called a disgrace when they have done something that deliberately hurts other people.

Grace is something that is hard to define. It is one of those things better understood when we see it in action, or even when we would expect to see it in action but instead see the opposite. Philip Yancey's bestseller, *What's So Amazing About Grace?*, opens up with the author recalling a conversation with a prostitute who was once asked if she would ever go to a church to get any help she needed. Her response was 'Church?! Why would I go there? They would just make me feel worse than I already do!'

Such is the unfortunate reality of much of Christianity in our world. Yancey points out the tragic irony that it was people just like this prostitute who flocked toward Jesus, not away from him. The worse a person felt about themselves, the more they found in Jesus someone safe, someone with whom they could feel totally accepted. How is it, then, that Christians have strayed so far from the teachings of their founder?

Maybe it has something to do with the fact that grace is something we just cannot get our heads around. Grace is generally defined as an undeserved gift. It is something done purely out of love, whether the recipient deserves it or not. For many people the world over, grace is not a word often associated with God. God instead is seen as a moral monster, someone who is so insecure that he needs his people's worship to make him feel better, or someone who is ready to smack you over the head the minute you do something wrong.

Grace, though, is the very characteristic that defines the God of the Bible, and is most clearly seen in the Jesus we see in the Gospels and expounded on in the rest of the New Testament. Jesus' life was characterised by grace, and many people couldn't handle it. One example of this is when Peter caught a huge load of fish after Jesus instructed him and his fishing mates to put their nets out into deeper water. Look it up. It's in Luke 5:1-11.

Peter's response in this story is typical of many of us. Why would someone be so extraordinarily generous to us when we have done absolutely nothing to deserve it? What do they want? But that is the very point of grace. It is not about ulterior motives. We are such a cynical society that we long ago lost the ability to simply trust in someone's goodness. Grace is not about getting according to what we have done. It is not about earning someone's favour, getting in God's good books.

Every one of you reading this, whether you are Christian, Buddhist, atheist, agnostic or whatever, is already in God's good books. The gift has already been offered to us. All we need to do is accept it. And that's the bit we find so hard - even so impossible - to comprehend. We just cannot get our heads around the idea that we actually don't have to do anything - anything at all - to get into God's good books.

In the end, grace turns the world upside down. When Israelis and Palestinians fight each other to the death, grace steps in and causes people on both sides to embrace in reconciliation; when Hutus and Tutsis in Rwanda come face to face with each other's families and their murderers, grace compels a mother with no children left to take in her family's killer and bring him up as her own son; and when people are dying of AIDS in Africa, grace doesn't even consider any judgments, but does all it can to save people's lives.

That is what is so amazing about grace. Through its strange operation in our lives, it transforms the world, both around us and within us.

The Eternal Question

If you could speak to God face-to-face, what is the one question you would ask, the one question that you have never been able to find a satisfactory answer for? For many people, no matter where they sit on the scale of belief, it is the question of how a supposedly good and loving God could allow such suffering and evil in the world.

It is a question that has bothered people for millennia, and it will continue to do so for millennia to come. Given that fact, we may be tempted to wonder what the point is of trying to come up with a solution. Shouldn't we just try to deal with suffering without wasting time on such existential questions as to why it happens?

The reason this question will not go away is because it goes to the very heart of belief in a Higher Being, and to making meaning of our existence. It is of prime importance to the human condition.

Throughout history, people have come up with all sorts of explanations to the question. Some of them are as follows:

- It is a natural consequence of what Christians call 'The Fall', that event in the Garden of Eden when Adam and Eve ate the forbidden fruit, resulting in sin, death and suffering entering the world.
- It is the judgment of God on sin. It seems that every time a natural disaster occurs, some preacher comes out and declares it as God's judgment on something that a marginalised group has apparently done wrong.

- There is no God, so what happens just happens and there is no explanation for it. Asking 'why?' is a silly question, akin to asking why we don't have square circles. As Richard Dawkins says in his book, *River Out Of Eden*,

    'In a universe of blind forces and physical replication, some people are going to get hurt, others are going to get lucky, and you won't find any rhyme or reason in it, nor any justice. The universe we observe has precisely the properties we should expect if there is, at bottom, no design, no purpose, no evil and no good, nothing but blind, pitiless indifference.'

- We can never know. If we could know all the reasons for everything that happens, we would be God.
- The original creation was deliberately not created complete. God wanted us to be co-creators with him. Genesis never says the creation was perfect; it says it was good. This is a view put forward by a number of people, including Terence Fretheim in a book called *Creation Untamed*.

Some of the above are reasonable explanations, but the one we can probably all agree on is that we can never know for sure. In the end our beliefs are held by faith – not blind faith – but faith based on reason – a 'reasonable faith' if you like. Everyone lives by faith, whether we are believers or not. Everyone has a worldview and there are some things we can simply never know. But the attitude we can have is that 'I am not going to let the things I'm not sure of take away from the things I am sure of'. Faith in the Jesus of the gospels is as reasonable as any other rational belief, probably more so.

Something else we can be pretty sure of is that suffering cannot be easily blamed on someone's sin. In John's Gospel there is a story of a man born blind who is healed by Jesus. The first response of Jesus' disciples is to ask who sinned that this man was born blind. As New Testament theologian N.T. Wright says, Jesus firmly resists any explanation like this. Just because something bad happens, it doesn't mean you have sinned in some way. The universe doesn't operate by karma; it operates by grace. Wright goes on to say, 'Something much stranger, at once more mysterious and more hopeful, is going on. The chaos and misery of this present world is, it seems, the raw material out of which the loving, wise and just God is making his new creation'.

This story of the healing of the man born blind is one of those incredible moments when God's new world is breaking in to renew this old, weary world. It is part of God's new creation coming into being. As John's Gospel says earlier, the light shines in the darkness and the darkness has not overcome it.

When we wonder why suffering takes place in a world made by a good and loving God, we are in good company. Jesus also asked why, and then said 'into your hands I place my spirit'. It was the ultimate act of trust that God is good and that goodness will triumph over suffering in the end.

Living a meaningful life is also an act of trust. It is done in faith that it is not pointless, but that it is contributing to a world that is coming, a world that will one day reflect the death of suffering and the victory of goodness. And it is done in confidence that God started the ball rolling one dark Friday afternoon on a rugged Roman cross, and then confounded the world by showing up alive again, the first fruits of this new world, on the most wonderful Sunday morning in history. That is the hope we have within suffering.

The God of Suffering Love

Many of us have probably seen Mel Gibson's *The Passion of the Christ* movie. When it was released in 2004, it caused quite a stir amongst different groups of people, not least for its gruesome and bloody portrayal of the torture that Jesus endured during the last twelve hours of his earthly life.

The word 'passion' has its origins in the Greek verb 'paschō', to suffer. So when we talk about the Passion of Jesus, we are referring to the suffering he endured, particularly during the last week of his life. In a matter of days, from the time that he rode into Jerusalem on a donkey, receiving wild acclaim from the crowds laying palm branches in front of him and hailing him as the coming King, to the utter humiliation of being crucified at the hands of the Romans, Jesus' life was turned completely on its head.

He knew his days were numbered, of course. The unfolding events of that tumultuous week came as no surprise to him. Luke 9 tells us that he resolutely set out for Jerusalem, telling his disciples that he would suffer and die at the hands of the authorities in that centre of power. His disciples were expecting him, as the Messiah, to overthrow the oppressive Roman regime, violently if need be. So for Jesus to speak about his upcoming death was something the disciples were simply unable to comprehend. No wonder Peter earlier rebuked him and said this must never happen (Mark 8:31-33).

While Jesus knew full well what he was up to, we also see, in all four Gospel accounts, that his attitude was one of service. That was in fact the very reason he was heading to his death, 'to serve, not to be served, and then to give away his life in exchange for many who are held hostage'. (Mark 10:45).

For his disciples, this required a complete change of mindset to understand what he was on about. The saying 'everything you know is wrong' was one they would have come to intimately relate to. And so, as they were squabbling over who would be the greatest in this new kingdom that Jesus was bringing in, Jesus turned it all around and said to them that if they want to be first, then the way to do it is to serve.

As always, Jesus walked his talk. By leading the way himself, he had the moral authority to tell his disciples that the way of life was the way of putting yourselves out there for others. And that inherently involves suffering.

A quick look at the news will remind us that we live in a world of suffering. Despite great progress towards poverty alleviation over the years, there are still 17,000 children under five years of age who die every day from poverty-related diseases. The Christian faith proclaims loudly and clearly that the cries of the poor are heard by God, for this is a God who has been in their shoes. God does not sympathise from afar; he empathises from within. We see Christ in the eyes of those who suffer.

This is God come to earth as a human person and walking in our footsteps. This is a God who says in the Garden of Gethsemane that he is troubled to the point of death, who is so anguished that he sweats drops of blood as he contemplates the incomprehensible enormity of what he is about to go through, all for love, all to make a better world in every way.

Who could imagine a God who is anguished, a God who suffers, and a God who, through all of this, serves? Is this not love at its best, continuing to give despite the cost?

The love of God gives us the strength to be the best we can be in our efforts to set the world right. Love shows us the way, love we see personified in the life of Jesus of Nazareth.

The Grace-Filled Life of Brennan Manning

Brennan Manning was an alcoholic. He was a drunk, a liar, a divorcee and an ex-priest who broke his vows to the Church. He is best known for his book, *The Ragamuffin Gospel*.

As a Christian, he was in good company. Moses was insecure, disobedient and a murderer. King David couldn't control his lust, abused his power to sleep with Bathsheba and then had her husband murdered to cover up his adultery. Saul the Pharisee (later Paul of Tarsus) systematically organised the murder of Christians in the 1st century.

You might not have heard of Brennan Manning, but you would have heard of the others. What do these others all have in common? You guessed it; they are three of the greatest heroes of the Bible. Yet look at their histories; all three of them were murderers. If that's all you knew about them, would you invite them over for dinner this weekend? Not sure if I would.

Despite these people's failings, God used them in the most dramatic, history-defining ways you could imagine. Moses stood up to the greatest power in the world of his time, the Pharaoh of Egypt, and led his people out of slavery to the Promised Land; David, the adulterer and murderer, came to be known as a man after God's own heart and was the greatest king Israel ever had; and Saul/Paul became the greatest disciple we have ever heard of.

These people were grateful recipients of grace. It didn't matter what they had done in their past. No matter our misdemeanours, our lives can be moulded by grace. When

God came to earth, Jesus lived out this life of grace. He said the prostitutes, tax collectors and other 'sinners' would go into the kingdom before the Pharisees, the ones who were so up themselves they thought they had the exclusive ear of God.

Back to Brennan Manning. Why was a man who was such a seeming failure at life so revered when he died some years ago? It was because in him we can all recognise our own failings. As Ben Simpson wrote a few days after Manning died:

'Those who identify with Manning relate to him precisely at the point he admits consciousness of his own brokenness, his own sin, and names his failings. Doing so gives others permission to do the same, to stop pretending, to come face to face with mercy'.

Here was a man who was acutely aware of his need for grace. He realised there was absolutely nothing whatsoever he could do to earn God's acceptance. His only options were dying an alcoholic death or clinging onto God's mercy. He grasped the latter option with everything he had.

Brennan Manning had an impact on literally millions of people the world over. He was one of the 'least of these' that Jesus speaks of in Matthew 25. Doesn't that just describe the very nature of God's kingdom? This is not a new world for the mighty and the powerful, for those who trust in riches and the stock market for their sense of wellbeing. This is a new world for the poor in spirit, for the humble, not the proud, for the ones who know they have failed and who are therefore amazed that the Maker of the universe would love even them.

These are the people who respond with gratitude for such grace and love. It is the insecure ones, the ones who realise that self-confidence is a liability because it gets in the way of God working in their lives, who are in fact the powerful ones. Theirs is a God-confidence.

St Paul's second letter to the Corinthian believers, especially the 12th chapter, is one of the most counter-cultural chapters in the whole Bible. Here Paul brags about his weaknesses. He attests that power is made perfect in weakness, and that 'when I am weak, then I am strong'.

Who in their right mind would brag about their weaknesses, except a person with a severely distorted sense of self-worth? But Paul knew the essence of being Christian, that it is not about being self-fulfilled, it is about the emptying of the self. Paul knew that it is in that that one finds strength, true self-worth and true strength of identity. This is what Jesus called building your house on rock rather than on the sinking sands of trying to find your life by filling it with things outside of yourself.

We spend our lives trying to earn acceptance, but grace says you are already accepted. This idea of trying to earn acceptance is so ingrained into us from birth that we literally cannot believe that we don't have to actually do anything to receive God's love. It is a gift that has been given to us. All we need to do is accept the gift.

Grace makes us realise that the world is a level-playing field, that no one is more superior than anyone else. Just because I wear respectable clothes, have a well-paying job, and live in a comfortable home in the leafy eastern suburbs, doesn't make me any more moral than the struggling drug addict living in public housing in the inner city.

In fact, just because I'm Christian doesn't make me any more moral than the staunch atheist. I am just one beggar telling another beggar where to find bread. When we do that we are pointing away from ourselves and pointing towards Someone other.

This Someone other, of course, is Jesus. In the end it's all about him. If we want to find out what grace looks like, what lack of judgmentalism looks like, what real strength looks like, we just need to look at Jesus.

This world is not a level playing field. Grace makes it so. No wonder Martin Luther King could long for a day when 'every valley shall be exalted, and every hill and mountain shall be made low, the rough places will be made plain, and the crooked places will be made straight'. King knew that this was what grace looks like. Like Moses of old, he passionately wanted what God wanted – a level playing field for his oppressed people.

Brennan Manning also knew what grace looked like. Oppressed by alcohol addiction, he knew that God's love extended to him just as much – no less, no more – than someone who has lived an exemplary moral life. In Jesus' way of looking at the world, it is people like Brennan Manning who are counted among the great ones.

The last are first in this new world order, the poor are given priority, and the outcast are given the best seats at the banquet. We are recipients of grace who get to dispense grace to people just like us. We are the most privileged people in the world.

The Great 'R' Word - Renewal

Most summers, we see the devastation of bushfires sear the Australian landscape as well as the Australian psyche. For many of us it brings back memories of the horrific Black Saturday fires of 2009.

Travelling up to Marysville – a town that was in the centre of the fires – a year after Black Saturday, it was amazing to see shoots of green coming through the blackened trunks of the burnt-out trees. There is something about nature that is life-giving. Life coming out of death; new coming out of old.

Standing there, you could imagine the fires racing through the forest on that terrible day, taking all before them, leaving nothing in their wake. Total destruction. But then you wonder: purely in terms of nature, is it destruction or is it part of the renewal cycle of life?

Christian faith is all about new beginnings. It says that Jesus is the beginning (and end) of everything – the Alpha and the Omega. And it is through him that all things are being renewed. Saying that seems hopelessly unrealistic, knowing that many of us are probably aware of people who have had their lives turned upside down by fires that ravish our country each summer. What, if anything, can Christian faith say when there is such devastation all around?

The theme of fire is one that is found throughout the Bible. When Moses climbed Mount Sinai and received the call from God to lead his people to freedom, God appeared in the burning bush; when the Israelites were then leaving Egypt, God appeared to them as a pillar of fire by night; and at Pentecost in the early days of the fledgling Christian movement, the Spirit is described as coming down as tongues of fire.

Fire is often associated with renewal in the Scriptures. The Spirit who came down as fire at Pentecost all those years ago is the One who empowers us to do the work of Christ in the world. The work of Christ is the work of renewal. This is the story that the New Testament tells, that from the coming of God into the world, through to the very end, a wonderful story is playing out – the story that everything is in the process of being renewed.

Entering a new year, we can be quite worn out after a stressful Christmas. To those who are struggling, Jesus says 'Come to me all you who are weary and heavy-laden and I will give you rest'. That's comforting news for a tired and weary world.

When we think of the horror of bushfires over our great south land, and the tragedy of other disasters in the world, it is enough to tempt you to despair. This is why, as we move further into the 21st century, the good news of Jesus is more relevant than ever. The world needs renewing, needs saving, and our celebration of Christmas is a remembering of the great news that a Saviour has come into the world.

Hope and renewal are what Christian faith is about. But the hope we have is not an insecure hope that may not eventuate; it is a hope based on the sure and solid fact of the physical resurrection of Jesus.

The signs of this hope are right in the midst of us. And what's more, we are renewed ourselves when we are part of something that is bigger than us. If we give ourselves to the cause of walking with Christ to renew the world, our lives will be shaped by the new beginning that matters above all else.

The Inherent Value of Work

Do you work to live or do you live to work? While the former is generally preferred over the latter, the idea of working to live – that we do our work and get paid enough in order to live a quality life – also needs to be challenged.

A long while back, our culture lost the belief that work on its own is beneficial to us. Work has inherent value in itself. Research shows us that it does wonders for our sense of self-worth. But at the same time, our confused culture gives us the mixed messages that, while on the one hand it is best for ourselves and the economy that as many people as possible have a job; on the other hand, when we have a job, we try to get away from it as much as possible. We live for the weekend or for that next holiday.

This innate desire to work to live reflects a Western-type dualism that splits work from the rest of life. In our society we talk about 'work/life balance', as if work is somehow separate from life. And while it is very unwise to drive ourselves into the ground by being addicted to our work, there is a problem with such dualistic thinking. It affirms the idea (although mostly unintentionally) that work is something to be tolerated - or even avoided - as much as possible for the more important cause of our life outside it.

Following Jesus in your workplace is about relationship, integrity, service, teamwork and growth. The reason this is so important is that it goes to the very core of our identity. The original creation act itself, as we read at the very beginning of the Bible, was an act of work by God. And the renewal of creation that we work towards reflects the creativity of the Creator. We are co-creators with God. In the creation accounts in Genesis, we see that God gives work to the humans before the Fall. God is a creative God and we are made in the image of God to continue to create.

This is why work can give us so much meaning, and why everything we do in life, including our work, matters. Richard Rohr says that the human soul can live without success but it cannot live without meaning.

We are given work to do for a purpose; we work for a kingdom that reflects the character of the King. This is also why everything we do in our work is to be done to the very best of our ability. God didn't look at the creation and say it was mediocre. God looked at it and said it was good. Excellence in our work is a witness to the character of God.

Any work that furthers the dream of God has inherent value in itself and is therefore eternally significant. May that fact strengthen your sense of purpose when you arrive at your desk each morning.

Was Jesus a Tree-Hugger?

When looking at a Christian response to the environmental crisis, we almost invariably focus on passages from the Old Testament. In particular, we look at the creation accounts in Genesis and explain how these have been misinterpreted in the past. We also might look at a few of the Psalms that talk about God being the Creator and Sustainer of everything in existence. But that's about it.

Do you see something missing in looking at the Bible this way? Who are we not mentioning when talking about the Christian concern for the planet? Here's a guess: it starts with 'J' and his name is contained in the previously mentioned word, 'Christian.' If you went to Sunday School you will know that the answer is always 'Jesus'. That's right; we often don't mention the central character in the whole biblical story when we proclaim our convictions about why Christians should be concerned for the planet. We genuinely wonder what Jesus ever said about creation, and we think we have to clutch at straws to try to convince ourselves that Jesus actually did have a concern for the natural environment.

Jesus stands at the centre of what the Bible is all about. That means that any strongly held assurances we have about the Christian mandate to care for creation must have Jesus at the centre. And it must have everything about Jesus at the centre – his life, his death, and his physical resurrection. Jesus didn't just come to die for our sins. Because of his life, death and resurrection, death has been defeated and all things are in the process of being made new. All things. That includes the environment.

We have seen previously that in Jesus' life, the kingdom of God was invading history. One of the most overlooked parts of Jesus' life that show his relationship to the non-human creation occurs in the opening lines of the oldest Gospel of all, the one written by Mark. It is no accident that Mark's Gospel (1:9-11) records that when Jesus was in the wilderness during his time of temptation, he was with the wild animals. Why would Mark mention this little detail? The New Testament scholar, Richard Bauckham, suggests that, in this case, Jesus 'is establishing his messianic relationship with the non-human world'. In the kingdom that Jesus came to install, all relationships are set right. Human, non-human, everything.

In an increasingly urban world where our lifestyles are more and more removed from nature and in which we increasingly try to determine our supremacy over nature, the stories about Jesus bring us back to reality. Jesus knew that humanity has an inherently embedded mutual relationship with nature. We are part of it. In fact, the Genesis creation account says that we were created out of the dust of the earth. As Jesus' God is the same as the Old Testament God, it logically follows that there is consistency in this area throughout the Scriptures.

Such mutual relationships are central to the kingdom of God. We are inter-linked with everything else on the planet. What affects one area inevitably affects others. You may have heard of the butterfly effect. Canadian environmentalist David Suzuki describes this in terms of the fact that ecology is increasingly teaching us that everything is related. He says that if all of humanity disappeared off the face of the earth, the rest of life would benefit enormously. The forests would gradually grow back, and relative stability would return to the ecosystems that control global temperature and the atmosphere. The fish in the oceans would recover and most endangered species would slowly come back. On the other hand, for example, if all species of ants disappeared, the results would be close to catastrophic. There would be major extinctions of other species and probably partial collapse of some ecosystems. The functions of the creatures living in the air we breathe, and beneath our feet, all work together to keep us alive. Remember that next time you're about to step on an ant!

What nature and the Bible show us is that a distortion of right relationships affects us, affects our societies and affects our environment. As Romans 8 tells us, the creation is groaning and awaiting the setting right of all relationships in the universe.

From creation to new creation, Genesis to Revelation, both nature and the Bible declare that God delights in renewal. And in Jesus we see this renewal lived out for us to follow. He is the ultimate environmentalist, coming to this planet to restore what has been despoiled and to set right all that has been wronged.

What does Prayer have to do with Poverty?

One of the distinctive marks of the Christian faith is the message that the God who made everything there is wants to have a personal relationship with us. God is both ultimate and intimate. When we look up at the stars on a clear night, we can often think like the Psalmist did:

> *When I consider your heavens, the work of your fingers, the moon and the stars, which you have set in place, what are mere mortals that you are mindful of them, human beings that you care for them? (Psalm 8:3-4).*

Pondering our existence in the context of the whole of creation can cause us to see ourselves as the famous astronomer Carl Sagan did, as a 'lonely speck in the great enveloping cosmic dark' - so tiny and insignificant that we just don't matter at all. Or we can marvel at the idea of that the One who made it all knows the number of hairs on our head (Matthew 10:30).

Christian belief affirms – loudly and clearly – the latter. God is personal, God is relational. We can know and be known by this God. And the way to get to know someone is through spending time with them, either in conversation or in stillness, just being with them. When we commune with God in this way, we call it prayer.

But how do we have a relationship with someone we can't see? And how do we do know if God is even listening and responding back to us? As St Paul said, we live by faith and not by sight (2 Corinthians 5:7). But it is not a blind faith. Our faith is what you might call a 'reasonable faith', one that is based on reason and evidence. And the clearest evidence we have of God speaking to us is, of course, the person of Jesus. If we want to know what God is like we can look at Jesus. Therefore, if we want to know how God views prayer, we need just look at the life of Jesus and the importance he placed on it.

There are about fifty references to prayer in the gospels. That would seem to suggest that Jesus placed a lot of importance on it. The gospels tell us that Jesus would at times spend whole nights in prayer (Luke 6:12), that he would go out at the crack of dawn to pray (Mark 1:35), would go by himself up a mountain to commune with God (Mark 6:46), and that he often withdrew from the crowds to pray (Luke 5:16).

In all the great work that Jesus did amongst the masses – bringing in the kingdom of God by his good works of healing, feeding the hungry, giving dignity to the outcast and oppressed – he backed it all up with prayer. Everything he did was grounded in prayer. The rest of the New Testament follows in Jesus' footsteps. St Paul tells us to pray without ceasing, and to always give thanks when we pray (1 Thessalonians 5:17-18). And in Acts we are told that the early church devoted themselves to prayer (Acts 2:42).

Prayer, for us, comes out of a recognition, conscious or otherwise, that we are not God and that we are limited in our power to affect the change we would like. This is why prayer is so crucial to our lives as disciples of Christ. We want to do everything that is possible to make the world a better place, but we recognise that we simply do not have what it takes to humanly make the changes we want to see. So we recognise that God is the ultimate change agent, that we are entirely dependent on God, that we want to love what God loves, and to want what God wants.

And what does God want? For this, we can look to another mention of prayer by Jesus, none other than the most famous prayer of all, the Lord's Prayer. The context of Jesus talking about the Lord's Prayer is that the disciples saw Jesus praying and asked him to teach them how to pray (Luke 11:1-4).

The Lord's Prayer is the greatest model of prayer for us. In it, Jesus addresses God personally ('Our Father'), he prays for God's reign of love, justice and transformation to be made real here ('your kingdom come on earth as in heaven'), he trusts God to supply our needs ('give us this day our daily bread'), he humbly asks for forgiveness just as we would forgive those who hurt us ('forgive us our sins, as we forgive those who sin against us'), he asks for protection from evil ('lead us not into temptation and deliver us from evil'), and finally, he humbly acknowledges that everything there is belongs to God ('yours is the kingdom, the power and the glory, forever and ever').

Genuine prayer is ultimately an expression of humility, which is itself an acknowledgment of reality, the reality that we are powerless in ourselves to affect all the change we want to. Jesus knew this too. He knew he had to rely on God, that he could do nothing except what he had been taught by God (John 8:28). Our lives are held in the palm of God's hand; we live in total dependence, and our prayer is an expression of this.

Prayer, however, was not only important to Jesus, but to many other people throughout the Bible. Jesus followed in the tradition of his Jewish heritage. His ancestor David has many of his own prayers recorded in the Psalms. Many of them are prayers of sheer exasperation at the state of existence, with all its corruption and injustice. Many a Psalm has David lamenting and crying out to God, 'how long until things are made right?!' David is unafraid to show his rage and anger at God for seemingly not doing anything and sitting by while the oppressors have their way.

David was known as a man after God's own heart, and his example shows that such can be our confidence in our relationship with God that we can yell and shake our fist at God; we can be brutally honest about how we feel, and our relationship with God is not at stake. God needs no defending; we have the freedom to come before God with all the raw honesty that our hearts can evoke.

Many of us are also inspired by the words of the Old Testament prophet Micah who said that God requires us to do justice, love kindness and walk humbly with our God. Many of us are often better at doing the first two – justice and kindness – than we are at walking humbly with God, which primarily involves a relationship with God that is based on much prayer.

Those of us who are more inclined this way, though, can take courage from the fact that prayer is also a counter-cultural act. This is again where we stand in the tradition of the biblical prophets. As the former National Director of World Vision India, Jayakumar Christian, says, 'prayer defies the cosmic powers that keep the poor powerless'. And Karl Barth adds that, 'to clasp the hands in prayer is the beginning of an uprising against the disorder of the world'. Prayer is an act of defiant subversion. When Jesus spent whole nights in prayer, these subversive acts clearly sustained him in his ministry, and they likewise sustain us.

When we pray for change in the world, we are saying that we are not satisfied with the way things are and that we want things to change. We are saying that we will not stop praying and petitioning God until we see change in the world. We will do all that is humanly possible, but knowing that that is not sufficient, we will seek help outside of ourselves, beseeching what 12 Step groups call our Higher Power, the One who can do what we cannot.

The vision of transformation we have for the world is not just for those living in poverty, it is also for ourselves and our neighbours here in the affluent West, that we will recognise that we too – perhaps we especially – need transforming.

Our prayer is also that God would work in us to have the will to help realise this vision. It is a tiresome task, but it is prayer that gives us the energy to continue when we are tired. Through prayer, God encourages us, gives us strength to continue the fight, to realise the vision of justice, peace and transformation that we long for.

Prayer is something that can be done in many forms. Most people in the world come from some sort of faith tradition. Most of these would be Christian, and some would be of other faiths. But the idea of prayer is fundamentally the same. It is about seeking God out.

The way we express our prayers is different for each group or even each individual. For many people, prayer is a ritual. It is good to have rituals because they give structure to our lives, and help us to live a self-disciplined life. For others, prayer is done loudly, in an atmosphere of something approaching ecstasy; while for others prayer is something that is more contemplative and quiet, done in the stillness of a small group or a Taize service. Each of these expressions has biblical foundations.

Whatever form our prayers take, they are essentially an expression of the human yearning for guidance, for help from outside of ourselves, and for relationship with someone Other. They are an act of faith, of trust that the One we are praying to is trustworthy and listens to us, despite what we may feel at times, and despite what we see around us. Our prayers are also an act of listening for that still small voice, of being still and knowing, as Psalm 46 says it.

This is why prayer is good for the soul. In our fast-paced 24/7 world where most of us are more connected than ever, we suffer from the lack of a soul Connection. Many of us suffer from what has been termed 'noisy souls'. We are so wired that we struggle to be alone with ourselves. This is where the old wisdom of Psalm 46 – being still and knowing – is so beneficial. It helps us to get back in touch with the Source of all our hope.

Throughout the whole of Scripture, we see the suffering heart of God for the poor and oppressed. Many of us have heard that there are over 2,000 verses in the Bible that speak about poverty. It is through prayer that we get in touch with this God who has a passion for justice and rightness. It is through prayer that we become more like this God who walked the dusty roads of the Middle East 2,000 years ago, giving his life that all might experience the joy of being part of the kingdom of love, justice and transformation that is coming. It is through prayer that our hearts are changed when we ask God, in the words of Bob Pierce, the founder of World Vision, 'Let my heart be broken by the things that break the heart of God'.

Your History Doesn't Have to be Your Destiny

'Cometh the hour, cometh the man', the saying goes (of course it applies equally to women but this is just a literal requoting).

This term refers to those who come through when they are needed most. For many of us, though, this statement can be quite discouraging. Some of us have failed at the most crucial times; we haven't come through, and we live with a gnawing sense of shame and self-loathing for years because of it.

For those of us who haven't come through when we have been needed most, this famous phrase can be used by us as a way of defining our identity. The good news, though, is that such a statement not only does not define us, but it is overshadowed by another, perhaps less famous phrase: 'your history doesn't have to be your destiny'.

Our past doesn't define us. We are worth much more than that. If we have failed those closest to us, we can, in our sorrow over what we have done, be reminded that our failure in no way changes our fundamental identity as people who are deeply loved and who have inherent dignity. Nothing, nothing in all the world, not even our worst failures, can take this away. St Paul says in his letter to the Romans that there is nothing in the whole of existence that can separate us from the love of God that we have seen in Jesus. Such a truth, when taken in, can change our lives.

John's Gospel has Jesus saying to his disciples that 'greater love has no one, than to lay down their life for their friends'.

These are not just the words, but also the actions of Jesus, demonstrated in his ultimate sacrifice for all of us in his life, death and resurrection.

Paul's letter to the Romans also says that it was while we were still denying God that he died for us. One of Jesus' closest friends, Peter, could relate intimately with this. On the night before Jesus died, it was Peter who denied he even knew his Master. Thinking only of himself, he pretended to the onlookers that he had never even seen Jesus before. It is, of course, when the rooster crows that Peter is confronted with the fact of failing his best friend. His bitter, painful remorse is then shown for all to see.

How would you have felt if you were Peter in that situation? You've just spent the best years of your life with the person your people have been waiting centuries for. He has chosen you to be one of his closest friends, he has stood up for you, affirmed you, and shown you a quality of life you never thought you deserved. But when *he* needed *you*, when the roles were somewhat reversed, you failed him. Can you imagine the shame of that? Can you imagine the bitter remorse?

For Peter though, and for us who have failed, it doesn't end there. As is his character, Jesus gets alongside Peter and restores him. It all happens in a strange little passage at the end of John's Gospel, after Jesus has been raised from death. Jesus is walking with Peter along the beach, and does something which seems really weird. He asks Peter if he (Peter) loves him. Peter responds, saying 'you know I love you'. No typical Aussie males here; these blokes know how to express their feelings!

But then, Jesus asks Peter the same question again, and then again! Three times! What is going on here? Is Jesus so emotionally insecure that he needs the affirmation of his best mate three times before he will believe it? Far from it. It is Jesus who is affirming Peter, not the other way around. The three questions Jesus asks correspond to the three denials from just a few nights before that would still have been playing heavily on Peter's mind.

Jesus knows Peter's heart; he knows that despite Peter's failures, he still loves Jesus beyond measure. And that is shown in the requests that Jesus makes of Peter. He gives Peter a job to do: look after the new Christian movement that would soon follow. Jesus was now trusting Peter, the one who had failed him so badly, to be a pillar of the new Christian movement.

Jesus had said earlier that Peter would be the 'rock' upon which his church would be built, and Roman Catholic tradition says Peter was the first Pope. He was a major player in the early church. Rather than getting him to step down because of his failures, Jesus told him to step up. This was affirmation, forgiveness and trust of the highest order. Peter had failed the Son of God so spectacularly, and what was Jesus' response? Jesus believed in Peter, and gave him a job to do.

What this highlights for us is that anyone is welcome to serve at the feet of this Jesus. We have all made mistakes over the years, but God still chooses to use us. That is not big-noting ourselves; it is actually cause for humility, that the Source of all justice would use even us to work to bring his justice into this broken world.

Your history doesn't have to be your destiny. Just look at Peter. He was restored, not just in the sense of Jesus saying 'there, there, it's ok', but also in the sense of Jesus giving him responsibility. Jesus believed in Peter, and he believes in us.

Restoration, transformation, renewal. This is the great story of The Gospel. Despite what your past may be, you can be restored, renewed and transformed, so that you can restore, renew and transform others. We are the most fortunate people in the world, and it is with this privilege that you can continue to fight for a world in which the love of God rules the day.

Recommended reading

Ash Barker, *Make Poverty Personal: Taking the Poor as Seriously as the Bible Does* (Baker Books, 2009)

Brennan Manning, *The Ragamuffin Gospel: Good News for the Bedraggled, Beat-Up, and Burnt Out* (Multnomah, 2005)

Brian D. McLaren, *Everything Must Change: When the World's Biggest Problems and Jesus' Good News Collide* (Thomas Nelson Publishers, 2009)

James M. Washington (ed.), *A Testament of Hope: The Essential Writings and Teachings of Martin Luther King, Jr* (HarperCollins Publishers Inc, 1990)

Jayakumar Christian, *God of the Empty-Handed: Poverty, Power and the Kingdom of God* (Acorn Press, 2011)

Larry Crabb, *Connecting: Healing Ourselves and Our Relationships* (Thomas Nelson, 2005)

Lisa Sharon Harper, *The Very Good Gospel: How Everything Wrong Can Be Made Right* (WaterBrook, 2016)

Mae Elise Cannon (ed.), *A Land Full of God: Christian Perspectives on the Holy Land* (Cascade Books, 2017)

Melba Padilla Maggay, *Transforming Society* (Wipf & Stock Publishers, 2011)

N.T. Wright, *Surprised by Hope: Rethinking Heaven, the Resurrection, and the Mission of the Church* (HarperOne, 2008)

John Smith, *Advance Australia Where?* (Anzea Publishers, 1988)

Richard Rohr, *Falling Upward: A Spirituality for the Two Halves of Life* (John Wiley & Sons, 2011)

Nils von Kalm

Richard Stearns, *The Hole In Our Gospel: What Does God Expect of Us? The Answer That Changed My Life and Might Just Change the World* (Thomas Nelson Inc, 2010)

Scot McKnight, *One.Life: Jesus Calls, We Follow* (Zondervan, 2010)

Walter Brueggemann, *The Prophetic Imagination, 2nd Edition* (Fortress Press, 2001)

About the Author

Nils von Kalm is from Melbourne, Australia, and has a passion for showing how the gospel is relevant to life in the 21st century. He has a Graduate Diploma in Theology, an Honours Degree in sociology and has taught on justice, poverty and development at the former Harvest Bible College in Melbourne. He also works in church and community engagement with Anglican Overseas Aid in Melbourne, and previously spent fourteen years with World Vision.

An avid reader and writer, Nils' interests are early Christianity, the person of Jesus, the question of God, and communicating how Jesus and the Gospels relate to every aspect of life.

You can connect with him on Facebook at https://www.facebook.com/nils.vonkalm and at http://soulthoughts.com/